AF351808

The WORK-LIFE ESCAPE ROOM

Choose to Stay or Choose to Move

Dave Silberman, Ph.D.

The Work- Life Escape Room

David Silberman

Tyler, TX

ds@worklifedisorder.com

Ordering Information:

Special discounts are available on quantity purchases by corporations, associations, educational institutions, and others. For details, contact David Silberman above.

Printed in the United States of America

First Edition

Softcover ISBN 979-8-88896-458-3

Ebook ISBN 979-8-88896-426-2

LCCN: 2024931979

Publisher

Winsome Entertainment Group LLC

Sandy, UT

The Work-Life Escape Room

I suggest that the time you spend at work is wrong; I also do not suggest anything in this book is right.

I have assembled 12 years of deep conversations about the time spent at work in my own life and what hundreds of other people have shared with me. Conversations that exposed the construction of a place many of us have been trapped within. Beyond helping you escape this place, should you choose to do so, my hope is this book helps inspire new conversations about the time life is lived at work and inspires new generations of people not yet working to no longer enter the place this book describes.

Acknowledgments

I am in debt to Bill Watterson, Stephen King, Rudolph Flesch, and Derek and Laura Cabrera. In different ways, their writing provoked and supported my courage to escape the place described in this book. Similarly to Joel Zimmerman and Jon Foreman, whose independent rhythmic genius each gave me grace throughout all the struggles and smiles as I wrote these words.

Preface

The Unintentional Truth

I never intended to write this book. I never imagined I would wake up one day exhausted of being exhausted from most of the time I lived my life at work. A part of my life I had invested most of my waking life building. The unintentional truth is that one day, for the first time, as someone who has always worked hard to build a professional identity, I could no longer see any glimpse of who I wanted to be. My response? Well, of course, do more the same, and what society, friends, and family have always supported us all to do. So, the cycle remained: move to another job, start another effort, do another venture. That is exactly what I did until the day I finally broke. On that day, I found myself throwing up every few hours and questioning everything I had ever done.

The story of how this book came about began in one of the darkest periods of my life. In a time when the most basic question, *"Who am I?"* overwhelmed me. Then, in my most desperate hour, I wrote, *"I no longer pride myself on my ability to take it, so I have to face it."* I realized I had sacrificed so much of my life living at work, not breathing nor being my best in any way I really wanted. I also began seeing through the facade all around me, reinforcing the idea that I wasn't the only one suffering.

As I fought through the darkness of that day, I began feeling overcome by hopelessness. A hopelessness I had felt and seen consume the lives of others many times before. A hopelessness that said, *"It is what it is; just learn to live with it and make the best of it."* In this struggle, a belief I once held strongly but had lost over the years reappeared. A belief born in my adolescence as I read the final scene of a young boy and his tiger going off into the snow. A belief that inspired me to believe:

It's a magical world.

I had lost this belief because I could never articulate how I could see it be true until a long-time dear friend and mentor (Sue Beecher) said the words that breathed life into what I struggled to say:

What would you do if nothing was impossible?

These words inspired me to write this book. While this book has rules and directions from many lived perspectives. I offer you my intent is not for this book to be something that "tells" you what is right and what is wrong; there is enough of that limitation in this world. Instead, I hope this book provokes you to reflect on the time you live your life at work and ask yourself if most of that time spent is living your life the way you really want? If not, I hope this book provokes and helps you begin moving to a place where you can.

I will never suggest this book contains all the answers to anything. This book expresses the insanity, vulnerability, and disorder of learning to breathe and be my authentic self. I hope you find it useful to help you arrive at a place where most of the time, most days each week, you can be happy, inspired, or fulfilled.

The Intentional Truth

The truth is simple mathematics and the shared lived realities expressed by society, friends, and family show people live most of their waking life at work, not happy, inspired, or fulfilled most of the time. Echoed everywhere and growing louder are claims, supported observations, and scientific evidence continuing to suggest the time life is lived at work is not serving the best of many. Burnout, disconnection, and horrible things are experienced daily by many hard-working people. I don't believe we need to continue discussing this negative reality or that many are not living as their best selves most of the time on most days each week - the evidence is overwhelming. Instead, what if we approached this part of our lives differently?

This book is a call to action for a new discussion in the working world about how we approach and spend time at work. A discussion focused on stopping the rationalized ridiculousness that continues to imprison and enslave people in the working day. I wrote this book to expose the manipulative puppetry used by the man behind the curtain, the conditioned consequences of a delusional dysfunction that has infected the working world with the madness of mediocrity, and to illuminate descriptive details of the obvious oblivious reality most of the time spent in waking life is enslaving lives away from being their best and getting what they really want.

My intentional truth is to awaken a day where the many, not only the few, are happy, inspired, and fulfilled, as they live their life in most of the time most days each week. A day that eliminates tragedies caused by egos, insecurities, and the regression of human potential caused by those addicted to power. A day that frees the authentic dreams and perspectives of eight billion and growing. A day of work full of possible impossibility that finds our world being its best most of the time.

Dare to be.–D.S.

Introduction

"...what the hell is water?" —*David Foster Wallace*

What would you do first if you just won $100 million? Quit your job? What if it was $50 million or $10 million? Still the same answer? Yeah, I thought so. Most people I have asked that question to for over a decade have said the same, and I did, too. Isn't it interesting? Of all the options that become instantly available with $100M, or with half or a tenth of that amount, quitting our job is often the first thing we say. Maybe that question is ridiculous, given the actual odds of winning that kind of money.

Instead, how about something you have now? The time you spend in your life at work in your head, heart, or hands, regardless of what day or hour. The time when work fills your life in and beyond your "official" working hours. Because let's be honest; it's not like work entirely falls out of you the minute you leave any given workday or workweek. Across your entire life, work will account for more time spent in your waking life than anything else. So, let's call this time your work-life. Would you say yours is ideal? One where most of the time you live your life at work brings you what you really want? The things you hold authentically true deep inside that find you happy, inspired, or fulfilled? Or would you describe your work-life like that only sometimes, or worse yet rarely? If the latter, don't worry; you are not alone. That is how I lived most of my work-life, too. And so did over 200 people whom I spoke with over a 12-year period. Many lived in different countries and were from different cultures and careers worldwide. People who shared intimate and intricate details with me about their work-life. People who worked as firefighters, freelancers, front-line workers, forepersons, engineers, executives, managers, and so many more.

Across these hundreds of stories, including mine, it became common to hear work-life described as if most of the time spent at work didn't feel ideal. Time could be imagined as being trapped in a prison. Spending most time awake in a place where fun was often missing and the time spent there felt monotonous, mundane, and sometimes even cold. And as each new day came about, more the same. The same time to start or go to lunch. The same time for meetings and when it was okay to leave. And should something more than more of the same be desired, it often meant going through lots of red tape. Yet, this lived reality was accepted through all the reflective stories shared. Some expressed their acceptance driven by fear, others as expressed frustrations, and still others from a position that anything different would be too uncomfortable. In common was an acceptance that sacrificing today *"is what it is"* because one day, someday, all these sacrificed days would add up and they could be free. All that needed to be done for that day to come was to survive and grind for years through the stress, suck, or saga routine. The routine that felt boring from sitting in meeting after meeting or having to deal with a co-worker or boss who felt compelled to start a rumor, make a ruckus, or be ridiculously rude for untrue reasons. And for some, the routine of feeling as if their soul was being sucked away most of the time. This lived reality didn't just exist most of the time in their work-lives or mine. It was also found in others we each independently knew. A reality so common it was familiar. Suggesting a work-life anything other than more of the same was not possible. Supporting the claims, many shared a work-life not more the same was one too good to be true and one only made possible for a few. I, too, felt similar. I lived trapped in this reality for decades. Pointing my life at work in a direction not on being who I truly wanted to be but instead who I felt I must be to survive. This might seem dramatic, but is it that far from your truth?

What if you considered the time you lived your life at work in a new way? A way where work was approached from a different direction? One that would allow the time spent at work to be different. Instead of rationalized ridiculousness that says it's normal for you to feel stressed out, burned out, and at times barely alive, move to a place where, most of the time, most of each week made you feel happy, inspired, or fulfilled. Living with a work-life you could feel as if it was meaningfully connected, purposeful, and impactful to getting what you really want. Impossible, you might say. I agree… Let me explain why.

I would like you to describe your ideal work-life. You might also think about it as time SpongeBob SquarePants might sing as "The best day ever!" at work. Time that brings you what you want at work and you wish you had most of the time. What does it look like? What are you doing while in it? How are you doing what you want to do the way you want to? Can you clearly describe all that right now? I say this respectfully and with no intended criticism; over a decade of asking that question, I have yet to have met more than a very few ready to describe all of that with little ease. However, what has been easy for many to share is story after story, describing how their life lived most of the time, most days each week, time spent in the stress, suck, or saga routine. So, I agree having an ideal work-life is impossible for you, me, and many of us. If we can't say what we want to see, there is no way for it to be. Given that reality, there is a better chance of winning the $100M. At least all the things that need to happen to win can be described. This, my friend, is the water we swim in. As David Foster Wallace once eloquently stated,

The most obvious, ubiquitous, important realities are often the ones that are the hardest to see and talk about.

The obvious yet oblivious reality is the new ways of work remain pointed in the old direction. A direction we have tragically grown numb to that brings harm to many most days each week. It's not the harm that is hardest to see and talk about. It is seen and talked about all the time. Harm that shows up like anxiety, depression, emotional exhaustion, hypertension, insomnia, social isolation, and many more. It's the reality where this harm is talked about over and over again. Yet, nothing ever changes except for more the same said in different ways. The reality many live in their current work-life is similar to the reality of accidents and deaths caused by speeding and drunk driving. Harm at work and harm on the roadways is talked about frequently. Still, more innocent people are hurt or killed each year alone by the harm we have grown numb to at work than in wars between nations that have occurred over decades. But don't you worry; something is being done about it. Everywhere you look, in your email, virtual meetings, and messages located in the halls and on the walls at the office, say so. The assholes are being sent to asshole training, and the next workplace survey will provide all the answers necessary to stop this harm, just like all those road signs, TV commercials, and annual reports. Constantly telling everyone not to drink and drive, don't speed; both hurt and kill.

How have we arrived at this reality? One where so many live most of the time at work this way? Especially given the fact you, me, and many others have spent tens, and in some cases, hundreds of thousands of dollars in education or had to shed sweat and tears for years in other ways to enter it.

Surprise! You, me, and many have been trapped in a game. Not just any game. Instead, like the popular board game you may have thought about. However, this game of life is your real life playing the game of work-life. And you are trapped in The Work-Life Escape Room. An obvious place where your current work-life lives most of the time, most days each week, not as you really want it to but instead in the stress, suck, or saga routine. A place you have lived so long it's oblivious to you there is any other possible way to play the work-life game. A place that trapped you from your very beginning with the stories, standards, and stigmas you have been told. A place not limited to trivial pursuits at the office but instead, a place where you play your game of work-life most of your waking life. It is an obvious yet oblivious place where I, too, lived for decades, and many, including you, still do. It is a nasty place that uses egos, insecurities, and power-hungry souls—incentivizing them each day to keep you inside until you have no more time to spend living and playing your game of work-life.

Like any game, The Work-Life Escape Room doesn't want you to win. It will nurture a work-life designed to keep you small to keep you within it. Some obstacles you must face are obvious, others not so much. Take, for example, the enlisted support of society, friends, and family, who, in many cases, have been unknowingly convinced to help deploy the game's twists, traps, and turmoil. A sample circumstance shared by many is one shared by Casey and Mirah. Two people living thousands of miles apart who never knew each other, even by name. Still, both had arrived at a work-life where they had what they once told themselves would make the time they spent at work ideal: more money, the title, and, in the case of Mirah, the office with the furniture. A progression praised by society, friends, and family. While both said confidently those things were nice, neither felt their work-life was meaningfully connected, purposeful, and impactful to being happy, inspired, or feeling fulfilled most of the time. And when both mentioned to their friends and family they wanted to leave and do something else, something common occurred. For Casey, his wife and mother disagreed and reinforced the importance of the benefits he had. Mirah found herself being hounded by her best friend not to overlook the time she had already invested and suggested all she needed to do was hustle more and grind harder.

What has been found in hundreds of lived stories, including mine, is the content that will be shared with you in this book. While all work-lives are unique, we are all more the same than different. The same obvious and oblivious puzzles and obstacles formed using comfort, fear, or frustration are what keeps many trapped inside. They are the things that stand in the way of escaping and living an ideal work-life. But for anyone who chooses to face and move beyond them, something many say is impossible awaits.

The Work-Life Escape Room is the immersive, live-action place where you currently live and play your version of the work-life game. What you face is a race against most of the time remaining to you in your waking life. The setting begins in The Misdirection—the reason why you, me, and many others have been trapped away from being happy, inspired, or fulfilled most of the time most days each week. Here, you will be presented with the backstory of the game and the conditioned reality and reasons why many choose to stay trapped. The game starts in The Chamber of Cerberus—a place where similar viewpoints are reinforced, and differences are suppressed. If you choose to move, you must face many obstacles. This includes The Beast That Keeps Us Within, The Madness of Mediocrity, and The Chains of Our Restraint. You must also learn to breathe and move through toxic air, being in the dark and feeling colder the more you move. To escape the chamber, you must ultimately find the clues and solve The Want-Day-Do puzzle. While it has been common for many before to escape this part of the room, what remains to be faced will only grow harder. As you enter The Den of Work-life Disorder, you will find time, feeling as if it is running out faster. You will immediately face the disorder that has kept you stuck between doing what you feel you must do to survive and doing what you authentically want to thrive alive. The tensional space of The Work-life Disorder has kept you, me, and many others from ever living fully present. To break free of this tension, you will have to find the clues necessary to solve The Priorities of Our Priorities puzzle. If you can complete this puzzle, you will then have to prepare to face the final two obstacles. These obstacles are often described as two of the three hardest in the room: The Monster of the Work-Life Escape Room and The Final Door to Escape. The time remaining in your waking life is yours to have or give away. What do you choose to do? Choose to stay or choose to move.

In the Work-Life Escape Room, there is no such thing as right or wrong, and fairness is not real. If you choose to stay, the consequences are yours to have. While I wish for a world where none remain trapped inside, the judgment of your choice is not mine or anyone else's to say. It's your choice. Common among those who have chosen to stay and live out their remaining work-life trapped inside are rationalized dissatisfactions, defended untruths, and self-justifications that claim to be the right reasons for believing an ideal work-life is impossible. With all of this in mind, the main question I give you is,

What would you do if nothing was impossible?

What lies ahead is not easy. It is the opposite of easy. Believing it will ever be easy is ill-advised. The way forward will only get harder until you escape. Your mission, should you choose to accept it is to:

Dare to be...

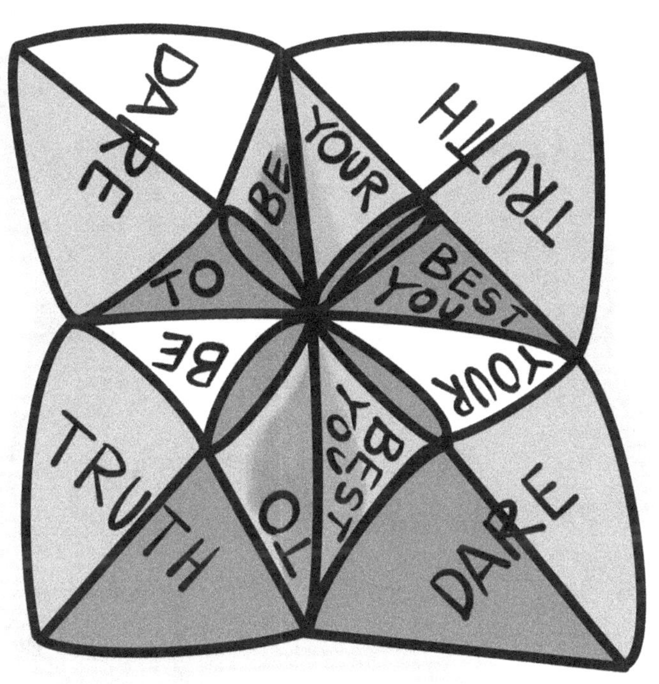

DARE
TRUTH
BE
YOUR
BEST
YOU
TO
BE
YOUR
BEST
TO
TRUTH
DARE

START
END

Contents

Part 1 - The Misdirection.. 15

Dare to Be 10

Part 2 - The Chamber of Cerberus.................... 33

Obstacle #1: A Three-Headed Dog Named Cerberus 35

The Beast That Keeps Us Within 38

Choose to Stay or Choose to Move 40

The Madness of Mediocrity... 44

Obstacle #2: The Madness of Mediocrity 45

Obstacle #3: The Chains of Our Restraint 50

You Already Are 53

Obstacle #4: The Want-Day-Do Puzzle 59

The Day You Made 64

Part 3 - The Den of Work-Life Disorder......... 65

Obstacle #5: The Priority of Our Priorities Puzzle.................... 67

Obstacle #6: The Monster of The Work-Life Escape Room 72

Obstacle #7: The Final Door to Escape 76

I Am Ready.. 80

DARE TO BE

IN ALL THE TRAVELS, DOWN ALL THE ROADS,
SOMETHING PECULIAR BECAME EXPOSED,
THROUGH ALL THE TITLES, THROUGH ALL THE MUSTS,
THE MOMENTS THAT MATTERED WERE MISSED OR RUSHED,
AND THROUGH THIS JOURNEY, IT BECAME EASY TO SEE,
THINGS WEREN'T MUCH DIFFERENT BETWEEN YOU AND ME,
YET IS IT SO CLEAR WE CAN SUBSCRIBE,
TO BE SOMETHING WE KNOW DEEP INSIDE,
AND WHY IS IT WHEN WE LOOK AROUND,
COMMON A PLACE SO MANY FOUND,
WORKING A JOB MOST DAYS OF THE YEAR,
THE BEST OF MANY ARE NOWHERE NEAR,
HOW IS THIS POSSIBLE IN ALL WE DO,
GO TO SCHOOL, TOLD WHAT TO DO,
WORK WE LIVE MOST OUR LIVES,
YET SOMEHOW WE HAVE NORMALIZED,
SURVIVING THE WORKDAY AS THE PRIZE,
BUT JON FOREMAN SANG IT DIFFERENTLY,
WE ARE HERE TO THRIVE, NOT GET BY,
THEN WHY ARE SO MANY WORKING EACH DAY,
BURNED OUT, STRESSED OUT, AND BARELY ALIVE,
IT'S NOT THAT WE CAN COMPLETELY IGNORE,
THE TIME WE SPEND INSIDE WORKS' DOOR,
NO MATTER HOW MANY DAYS AWAY WE GET,
NEVER AWAKE MORE THAN AT WORK SPENT,
NOW IN THE WORLD, OVER EIGHT BILLION AROUND,
AND STILL, NOWHERE A REPLICA OF YOU FOUND,
SO WHO OF YOU WILL YOU CHOOSE TO BE,

WHO OF YOU DO YOU WANT TO BELIEVE AND BREATHE,
MY HOPE FOR YOU IS TO CONSIDER,
THERE'S MORE OF YOU TO DELIVER,
AND IF THIS TRUTH YOU BELIEVE AS WELL,
YOU MUST BE PREPARED TO MOVE YOURSELF,
NOT AS THE ONE WHO WILL SACRIFICE,
OR CONTINUE ONWARD WITH COMPROMISE,
INSTEAD, BE THE ONE WHO WILL BE TRUE,
THE WHO OF YOU THAT IS THE BEST OF YOU,
YOUR UNIQUE POTENTIAL CAN ARISE,
BUT ONLY IS POSSIBLE THROUGH YOUR EYES,
HOWEVER, YOUR DREAMS REQUIRE MORE,
THEN THE ACT OF BELIEVING YOU WILL SCORE,
WITH COURAGE, YOU MUST MOVE AWAY,
FROM MANY THINGS, YOU WILL WANT TO STAY,
CHALLENGES AHEAD UNDOUBTEDLY WAIT,
YOU, YOURSELF, THE GREATEST RESTRAINT,
AND OTHERS WILL NOT EASILY AGREE,
WITH ALL THE THINGS YOU WISH TO BREATHE AND BE,
WHAT'S AT STAKE IS NOT THEIRS TO SAY,
IT'S YOURS TO GET OR LOSE AWAY,
AND ONLY IF YOU DARE TO MOVE,
A CHANCE YOU HAVE TO LEAVE THE ROOM,
THE ONE RESTRAINING YOUR BEST SELF,
THE ONE THAT'S LIKE NO ONE ELSE,
BUT IF YOU DARE TO GO OUTSIDE,
BE PREPARED TO REALIZE,
EVERYTHING YOU NEVER THOUGHT COULD BE,
DARE TO BE AN IMPOSSIBILITY.

The Rules to Escape

12

Rule #1 No choice is right or wrong, and fairness is not real. It is either authentic to you, or it is not.

Rule #2 No choice is right or wrong, and fairness is not real. It is either authentic to you, or it is not.

Any guess why #1 and #2 are the same, and need to be said twice?...

Rule #3 Where you look is where you can choose to move and go.

Rule #4 If you don't write it down and say it out loud, whatever it is will never become in your lived reality.

Rule #5 You can never go back or forward the same way you came.

Rule #6 You do now and will always contain something no other human can.

Rule #7 No work-life is more important than any other.

I won't wish you off without one last warning. It has been said by many before once you can see The Work-life Escape Room, its reality can never be unseen. A few have said the journey out of the room was scary, confusing, and unsettling. This is because The Work-life Escape Room is not a place that wants you to leave. What lies ahead is not comfort, confidence, or support. Instead, you will be distracted by distractions designed to deceive you. Choosing to move is a choice to move through many twists, traps, and turmoil. Everything you are about to face will seek to convince you anything other than more of the same is wrong. Many will try and stop you from leaving. Including those you may trust or look up to in society or among your friends or family. Yet nothing can stop your escape if you continuously choose to move.

If you accept this mission, let's begin…

The Misdirection

"Some things are believed because they are demonstrably true. But many other things are believed simply because they have been asserted repeatedly." —Thomas Sowell

Work to live or live to work, the debate about which is better misses the point. We live in a society where the time spent dreaming, thinking, and being a job is greater than most time spent elsewhere. In the end, despite who you are, where you live, or what you do, you will live most of your waking life at work whether you work six, eight, or 18 hours a day, four, five, or six days a week. Yet, many cannot describe most of the time they spend at work as time they find themselves happy, inspired, or fulfilled. Instead, work is often described as something that must be done to survive and pay the bills. Look at the stories shared about work-life between people who meet up in restaurants and bars or those who sing songs like 9 to 5 by Dolly Parton. If you happen not to be familiar with this song, it is a song with lyrics that describe work-life as time spent barely getting by and most days each week as sacrificing oneself only to make other people richer. Let's not forget about similar stories described in movies and TV shows. Like from the pop culture hit movie Office Space, whose character named Nina, portrayed by actress Kinna McInroe, had a stereotypical lack of enthusiasm about the beginning of the work week, expressed in the line *"Looks like someone's got a case of the Mondays."* Or words shared by comedian and actor Drew Carey, who once said, *"Oh, you hate your job? Why didn't you say so? There's a support group for that. It's called everybody, and they meet at the bar."* The common stories of work-life describe time spent at work as time we dread to spend, as time filled with rampant boredom, or as time spent at a place where happiness and joy are only found when leaving work each day or when the week at work has come to an end. It is a sentiment so true a popular restaurant captured it and used it as its name. A restaurant you may know as T.G.I. (Thank God It's) Fridays.

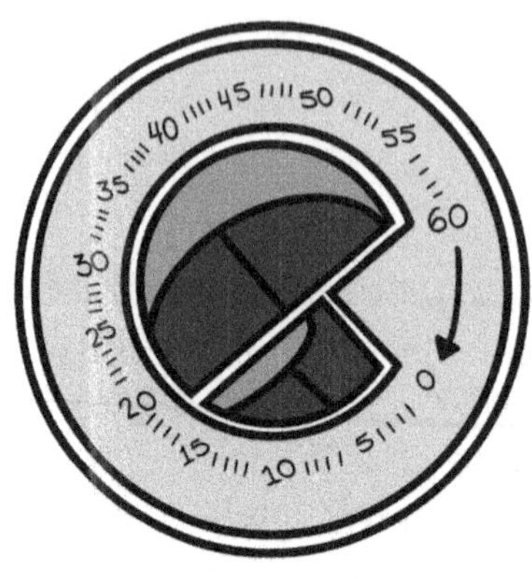

The current work-life many live in often starts with, *"I gotta get this job because I gotta survive."* So, what happens? The job hill is charged like The Little Engine That Could where people think and repeatably say, *"I gotta survive, I gotta survive, I gotta survive."* Guess what happens? Many go to work and strive to survive. In the strive to survive pursuit, the idea of a good enough work-life becomes attractive. So much so that it is often thought of as the thing to have. To get a good enough work-life all that is required is to survive the time you live your life at work. Here lies the crux of the problem. A good enough work-life can indeed be good enough. But time spent at work that is only good enough will not bring anyone what they really want most of the time. Yet, a good enough work-life is what is often promoted and celebrated. This reality has shaped the common belief many share that having an ideal work-life is impossible.

I know what I said doesn't seem right. The truth about work-life is there is no such thing as right or wrong, and fairness is not real. The system that created the space your current work-life lives does what it was designed to do. And it will continue to do what it does in a direction not concerned with what is best for you. So, it's time to face this restraining truth. Your work-life is trapped inside The Work-Life Escape Room. And while your work-life remains trapped, the best it can be is good enough. Having a good enough work-life means you can get what you really want and be happy, inspired, or fulfilled some of the time. This means you get to have something else during most of the time. The reflection on my own work-life and stories shared from hundreds over twelve years suggest when living in a good enough work-life what fills up most of the time is the stress, suck, or saga routine. This routine is as reliable as morning traffic, experienced most days each week. A routine lived in for 20, 30, or more years. All in exchange for the chance one day someday to live life for 10 or 20 years where most of the time life can be lived the way it is truly really wanted.

The delusional dysfunction that says living most time at work in the stress, suck, or saga routine, feeling uninspired, unhappy, or unfulfilled, has been normalized for decades and generations. And so has the undue impact it brings upon the quality of life as routinely talked about in the news, in restaurants, in bars, and at the dinner table with friends and family. Day after day is more the same, yet for many, this is how most time at work is expected to be. My intent here is not to start with something sad. But to continue ignoring the obvious oblivious reality robbing many hard-working lives most of the time in their waking life from feeling happy, inspired, or fulfilled is sad.

The way you, me, and many others were taught to play the game of work-life trapped us in The Work-Life Escape Room. In our earliest days, long before our official work-life began we were exposed to a code. No, not the up, up, down, down, yada yada gaming code many know. But a code that came from the stories, standards, and stigmas we were told to think about when we thought about what we would do when we grew up. A code that starts with:

Once upon a time go be a job…

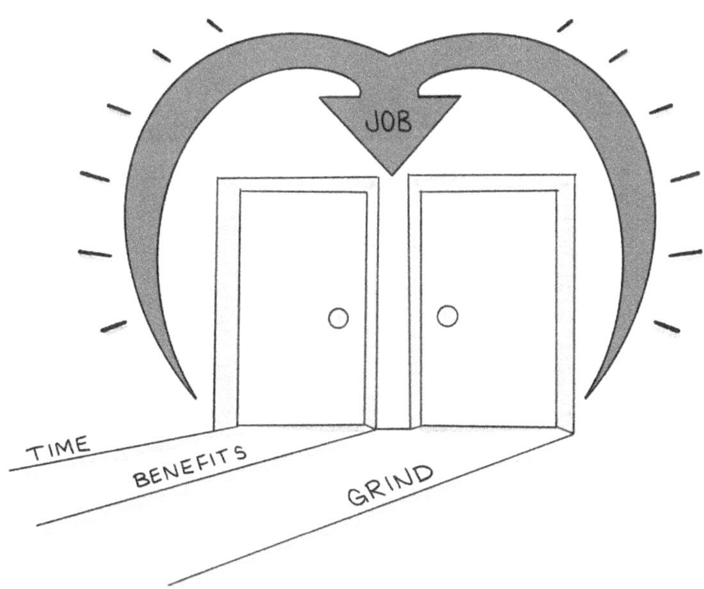

Our eyes were first taught to gaze at the time spent at work as young children. Our parents, grandparents, or people who we saw as influential would often read us stories and share their ideas about what we could be when we grew up. Can you remember at a young age hearing thoughts about being a doctor, a fireperson, a teacher, or what it would be like to spend time from your life at some job? I can remember my early love for the idea of space and how my fascination encouraged many around to prompt me to think about being an astronaut. From a very young age, not even eight years old, I told my Granny I wanted to drive a car on the moon. Other grownups supported my wonder and would tell me things they knew about space or had recently learned. How time mainly was experienced at work also showed up in many cartoons I watched, and you might have, too. Did you watch The Jetsons, where George Jetson worked for Mr. Spacely and Spacely Sprockets? Or Scooby-Doo, where the gang spent time at work as detectives solving crimes. Or what about The Smurfs and all the different jobs in their village? And what about Bob, the builder, and his team of machines spending time of their life working in construction? Or the famous SpongeBob SquarePants and his love for making Krabby Patties while working at the Krusty Krab. Remember how I told you about my passion for space? My sense of wonder and dreams about it was only magnified when I discovered Bill Watterson's characters Calvin and Hobbes and the adventures of Calvin's alter ego, Spaceman Spiff.

As we got older, our exposure to the time spent at work expanded. For me, this started with spending time with my Papa. Papa was a farmer, and I spent a significant amount of time in my childhood with him working on the farm. Decades later, I can still remember what it was like sitting on the armrest of the tractor, watching him for hours as we went up and down many fields, preparing them to grow many different things. When we weren't in the real tractors, I remember playing with toy tractors and plowing the carpet fields I imagined in the living room or basement of the house I grew up in. As I grew old enough to drive the real tractors, I remember always trying to plow the fields as perfectly as I saw my Papa did. I also still, to this day, can feel what the summer harvest felt like. There was an urgency and expectation about how time should be spent during the summer harvest of everyone who stepped onto the wheat field.

During summer harvest, there was a rule. It is fair to call this rule the most important rule. The rule that said the combine never stopped. Well, except to refuel. When that occurred, an important rule was added. Clean the windows on the combine fast and so well that it would be hard to believe it had windows at all. But besides that, the rule *"the combine never stopped"* was the most important.

I distinctly remember one evening working summer harvest with my cousin Shelli, one of my best friends growing up and, to this day, a person who remains one of the most underrated people I know. She and I had to leave the wheat field we were currently working on to take something over to where the harvested grain was stored. It was on the way back when the inevitable happened. Sooner than we expected, our Papa turned on the hazard light flashers of the combine. This was the signal the combine needed to be unloaded. A process where we needed to drive another tractor alongside the combine while it remained moving to allow the most important rule to be followed. We were so far from the tractor we needed to jump in. I am still confident to say I don't believe either has lost our breath, requiring a larger gulp of air since we faced that moment of despair. We had to get across what felt like 100 miles when, in reality, it was just a few fields, including one field full of freshly baled hay. Shelli and I still both vividly remember that moment when the urgency instilled by our Papa compelled me to drive at speeds not safe for regular roadways, weaving in and out of hay bales scattered on the ground. What did this have to do with my exposure to how time should be spent from life at work? It told me time spent working hard was important. And spending that time hustling through a grind mattered. These directions have influenced how I have played the game of work-life most of my life. You may have had something similar or different. But can you reflect on any time during your earlier childhood when you were exposed to how time at work was expected to be spent?

As a teenager, I was allowed to engage my curiosity, which shifted away from space and onto police officers. I know I was privileged not to have some of the exposure to the police you may have. My exposure impressed the idea that police officers were focused on helping others. An idea first inspired on a day I saw a police officer help another kid who was severely hurt by a rock thrown by another kid that hit her in her eye. As my exposure increased, so did my impression of police officers, which further suggested their job meant spending time at work focused on helping others. Over and over again, I was privileged to be exposed to police officers who routinely put their lives and safety on the line with the intent to help others. People like Officer Mark Ashby codified a belief that spending time at work as a police officer meant having love, care, and concern for other humans, strangers or not. Officer Ashby's impression directed my thoughts, dreams, and efforts regarding what job I wanted to spend the time of my life doing. You have permission to laugh; a version of my senior pictures was taken in my police cadet uniform. Maybe you had different opportunities and experiences. But can you reflect on people you engaged with during your teenage years and how they may have influenced how you have chosen to spend the time in your life at work?

As we progressed through our teenage years, the noise from society, friends, and family about spending time from our lives at work increased. Not only about getting a job but what job we would get. I can vividly recall how often I found myself pulled into conversations focused on convincing me how important it was to get a job where I could get the benefits, put in the time to earn more, and hustle and grind to earn titles and promotions. These similar themes were echoed by my teachers in their feedback from the inevitable *"what do you want to be when you grow up"* assignments. All these influences suggested if I focused on being the right job I would find happiness, inspiration, and fulfillment living in my work-life. One that would be good and routinely express joy similar to how you might see a young child on the day they got the puppy they always dreamt about.

Then the day arrives, and the official time in work-life begins. We go and be a job. The job we already spent lots of time thinking about, talking about and investing time from our life to get. The early days being a job are often chaotic but exciting. And as the first years go by, more the same. Getting to live all the things that came with being the job we worked so hard to be. Everything usually goes great until the day it doesn't. For some, it was a boss who finally pushed them too far. For others, it was looking one day in the mirror, saying they hated their job. And still, for many others, it was many other things. Stacie shared how she was always told to ensure she could make ends meet. And that is what she did day in and day out. She would work one job during the day and another at night. She shared how one Monday afternoon as she was shifting from her day job to her night job she felt as if she was going nowhere. Stacie shared she was filling gas into her car and as the amount went past $75 she said to herself, *"I am working so hard, and yet it feels like all I am working for is to put gas in my car."* Elizabeth went to be a job guided by the support she could find. In our conversations, Elizabeth highlighted how she wanted to become a marine biologist but ultimately became an attorney in the state system.

Elizabeth, with that choice, found lots of support from her friends and family. But then on a day that would be expected to bring joy, a day Elizabeth found herself getting promoted she shared how she realized how bored

she had become. Elizabeth shared the story that while at her promotion ceremony she remembered staring out one of the windows and watching the trees and little birds flying around. To her, the promotion would only bring her more work and not the opportunity to feel happier, inspired or fulfilled while spending her time at work. Isaac shared how he grew up in a foster home and could never get a good break. He felt lucky to have the job he held during our conversations, but shared he wanted more for himself and felt having more was only for someone else. Common to these and most of the stories shared with me for 12 years was the day many realized their good enough work-life was not bringing them what they wanted. It has been commonly observed in many, including me, when waking up in this day, there is a strong feeling to look around as if the answers needed to change this day would be found in others. Yet, in many cases, the people sought out are also trapped inside The Work-Life Escape Room. And because we often are unable to see this reality, there is a common comfort and confidence to grab on tightly to their words and advice. With those sought perspectives in hand, we move our hearts, hands, and minds back into the workday, thinking we are moving in a new direction. One that will bring us to what we really want from the time we live our lives at work. All while not realizing we have just breathed in a madness that will help convince us to stay trapped inside The Work-life Escape Room. A madness that acclimates us to this imprisonment like a frog being brought to a boil in a pot of water.

I may never forget the day this happened to me. I was in a downstairs hallway of the police department. A hallway I had walked up and down for years. It was the hallway that led to the locker room to get dressed, the briefing room to get prepared, and the one that led to the door to start the day. This moment hit me as I opened the door to start my day. A door that always felt a little overdone by its weight and size. It was then that an overwhelming feeling came over me about the job I had wanted to have for as long as I could remember. I realized I was spending my life at work not breathing or being all of who I wanted to be. In a mild panic, I did what could be expected. I looked for others who worked where I did and whom I looked up to for many years. And as soon as I could, I chased them down and asked them for directions. In almost a uniform fashion, I was told I was looking at work all wrong and I needed to learn to play the game the way the job prescribed. If I did, I would go far. Do you have any guesses on what I did in response to all that direction? Exactly. I listened to that advice, soaked it up as much as possible, and did my best to apply it. I learned the rules of the institution, the babble of the bureaucrat, and what was fashionable in organizations and what was not. And I followed that advice for decades.

At this point, it is fair to think these stories are nothing but typical stories of growing up and moving through a career. Exactly. Typical stories, more the same than not, even when described in different ways. Stories that find you, me, and many others spending the time in our work-life most days each week acclimated with the stress, suck or saga routine. Working hard each day where what is possible is limited by concessions and sacrifices.

Telling ourselves reflections such as *"I can put food on my table"* or *"I can be healthy"* or *"I can get the promotion and run the company"* or *"I can be present at most of my kid's games or recitals."* And of course, the all too familiar reflection that says, *"I have to put in my time at work even though I don't like most of it most days each week, but one day someday I will have what I want most of the time."* So, what do you do if you want something different than more the same? You must escape.

When you are trapped in The Work-Life Escape Room your ability to see is constrained and disoriented. You no longer focus on who you are inside or what you really want from most of the time you live your life at work. Instead, you look and move to what you see on the outside and what you are told should be. In doing so, you walked yourself, like many of us before, into the crowds playing the counting game. Here, you are surrounded by society, friends, and family, all placing bets and making measurements on most days. The names of those with the highest scores are chanted loud and proud. As if the ones with the highest scores are considered better than all the other people. How does anyone get the highest scores? By getting most of the points from what society, friends, and family say count. Points earned in one of three categories. The first come from the benefits of the job. Points in this category are often counted by the money that can be made. Next are the points that come from putting in the time. Points that incrementally come the more time at work is spent over the years. Finally are the points found in the titles and promotions connected to the hustle and grind. It has been a common belief to earn points in this category means sacrificing time away from friends, family or sleep. I am not saying that getting the benefits of having a job, working for most of your life, or working hard to earn titles and promotions are bad. I am saying focusing on only those things are what keeps many of us trapped inside The Work-Life Escape Room. When we put what counts over what matters, what matters no longer counts. My next question to you is:

What counts for what matters to you in your ideal work-life?

I always had big dreams, and as I got deeper into my career, those dreams only grew. With no intent in sounding arrogant and fully recognizing this may, I got tired of seeing people around me have everything I wanted and asked myself, *"How are they better than me?"* So, I looked at them more. I saw some had gone to school, so I got a Ph.D. I saw some had put themselves in executive clubs, so I put myself in the C-Suite. And I always saw some at work. So, I, too, put myself at work 10, 12, and 16 hours a day, mostly six but often seven days a week. And what score did I get by telling myself, *"this is what I should do?"* A decent one if rating myself in the counting game against many of my friends and peers. I travelled to many places and had many successes. Yet, in the midst of the relentless hustle and grind of work, I focused solely on racking up points. My life became consumed by the demands of the job, leaving little

room for anything else. I worked so many hours each week all my body could do beyond eating and sleeping was become obese. Over time, I gained 54 pounds and struggled to relate or participate in doing anything outside of work. I was usually too tired, and the stress from doing what it took to get the highest points made my everyday mood uninterested in doing anything else. The day I broke, something interesting occurred. I realized I was so busy chasing what I was told by society, friends, and family that I was no longer pursuing my dreams; the real ones, the ones meaningfully connected, purposeful, and impactful to what the bigger me inside really wanted. Living the time in my life in constant adventure, being authentic, and thriving alive. As I continued to face that day, I began to see the ones I was looking at, the people who I told myself I should be like with their swimming pools, big bank accounts, and power could have nothing more. They achieved the top of the counting game, and many would ooh and ahh about them. They had exclusive access to many impressive places. And while committing their life to achieve all the things that counted, I began to realize what mattered to them didn't matter to me. What was authentic to me and the score I wanted was something different.

The real me, the person who, like you, is unique and unrepeatable, given the fingerprint on each of our hands, didn't want more of the same. But I did not realize that until the day I broke. I had spent over two decades focused intensely on doing my best to get the most points that society, friends, and family said counted. And while I scored lots of points, I wasn't free. I wasn't having fun, and the person I saw in the mirror each day wasn't the person I wanted to breathe and be. Before we move on, I ask us to pause as I restate something so obvious it may be oblivious. Nowhere in the official scoring of the counting game or the position descriptions you, I and many were told to go be is the word *fun*. As if the time in our life wasn't short enough already.

What about you? What have you been telling yourself to chase? Have you ever found yourself like me or the hundreds who I spoke with for over a decade? Using what was around you as a guide to live your work-life? Across all the conversations, it was frequent to see many, including me, say something like, *"If I can make the same money as Michelle, I would have all I want."* But is what it means to make the same money as Michelle obvious? As you consider that question, let me offer you a brief story about my time chatting with Brett. Brett saw all the things Corey had and felt he also wanted them. This was the time Brett had in his mind that if he could make the same money and get the same promotion as Corey, he would have all he needed, and all his struggles would disappear. But Brett shared he had discovered something along the way. A discovery that ocurred the day he worked up the courage to ask Corey for advice. While he was listening to Corey, rigorously writing everything Corey was telling him, he saw something unexpected through his scribbles. Corey was sharing what he did over the past two

years that brought him the increased money and promotion. What he didn't say is what caught Brett's attention. When Brett asked Corey about what he didn't say, Brett told me he had heard seven words he believed he will never forget. Brett asked Corey how he could accomplish what he had just described while taking time away from work. You see, Brett promised his wife and kids the day his youngest son was born that they would take a big vacation every year. One that he had never missed and had no desire to ever miss. When Corey told him seven words, Brett described his feelings inside as if the lights had just come on in his mind for the first time. Corey told Brett, *"You have to choose what you want."* Followed by lengthy justification defending what it took to stand out from the others trying to get the same money and promotion. While Brett wished he could make the same money and have the same promotion as Corey, the cost wasn't worth it. Brett's 40-hour-a-week job gave him the energy to be present in things he felt counted to what mattered to him. In the ten years he had been working in his current job, he could only think of one or two times he ever had an issue taking days off or getting approval for the specific days he wanted. And guess what? While on the surface, it would appear Corey might be viewed as someone only seeking money and promotion at work, there is more to his story. As Corey grew up, he saw his father constantly work, yet routinely be overlooked for promotions. At the time Corey and I spoke together, his father had already passed away years prior. What counted to what mattered to Corey was making it to the top as vindication for his dad. I am sharing Corey's story with you as context for this game. Corey's story represents an example of someone being trapped for the right reasons. And it wasn't until Brett introduced Corey to me that I could see how numb we can become to the delusional dysfunction of the counting game. I asked Corey the same question I asked you:

If you had to describe your work-life, would you say you are happy, inspired or fulfilled most of the time?

When I asked Corey this question, he looked at me with eyes energized to seek clarity and communicate conviction when he said, *"What are you talking about? I am the Senior Vice President over a portfolio responsible for hundreds of millions of dollars; I love my job."* As we conversed more in one of the most beautiful corner offices I have ever sat in, I asked Corey, *"Are you who you dreamed you once would be?"* His response was, *"I'm more than that."* As we talked some more and he showed me around his office and the breathtaking views overlooking the bay from the magnificent windows making up an entire wall, I asked Corey one last question, *"Does the time you live your life at work bring you what you really want deep inside most of the time?"* Through a pause that was only seconds but felt like minutes and a with a gentleness I hadn't heard in his voice the entire time, Corey told me, *"Dave, you can't have all."*

Indeed, in the current work-lives of many, what Corey said highlighted a common reality. A reality justified by the right reasons. We can concede our lives in ways we may not see when we get sucked into the crowds playing the counting game. Yet, this reality is often oblivious when we get frustrated and say, *"If I could only make the same money as Michelle or Corey, or when I get that promotion, I will have all I want, and all my struggles will disappear."*

The top scorers in the counting game are given lots of attention. They can be found filling jobs as CEOs of Fortune 500 companies, professional athletes, accomplished members of Hollywood, foreign leaders, members of the U.S. Congress, and others similar in terms of power, wealth, and status. Indeed, scoring high points in the counting game brings access to many things. But if being a top scorer brought with it all that matters (as the crowds playing the counting game try to convince), then how can top scorers be so frequently found addicted to antidepressants, alcohol, or other alternative distractions? And if those examples are just thought about as a consequence of people having too much money and being bored, then what about those top scorers who have explicitly come out and said the time they live their life at work has brought them real harm? And said with no judgment, what about those top scorers who have been convinced to take their own life? This is not to say these things only happen to top scorers in the counting game. It is to say it is both interesting and irritating how society, friends, and family endorse a 'counting game' that values only certain achievements; and yet those who succeed at the highest level of those achievements have also frequently been found to be unhappy, uninspired, and unfulfilled.

How about we be more practical to the world in which you and I have lived most of our work-life. What about examples of those playing the counting game but have not yet achieved its top scores? Let me share a brief story about my time chatting with Aisha. She grew up in a home where little money existed. She was a hard worker from a very young age and carried grit in everything she did. Day in and day out, she would always get done what needed to get done. Even at times when that meant not playing with friends after school so she could help her mom sweep floors at a local grocery store in the evenings or on the weekends. When she spoke with me, she was starting her sixth year at work. She hadn't yet made the money she wanted from her main job, so she babysat kids in her neighborhood on the weekends and worked as a janitor at night. Having spent much of my life working three or more jobs, I asked her how she felt. She told me she was mostly exhausted most of the time but had more money than anyone in her family ever did. Similarly, I met Jeff, who also felt earning as much money mattered greatly to him. But unlike Aisha, who openly said she was exhausted yet believed the hustle and grind of getting the money she wanted was worth sacrificing other things, Jeff felt something different. He also worked long hours but found himself in what he described as daily guilt and tension. On the one hand, he was making more money than he ever thought possible, and on the other, he was too exhausted most days to be present with his kids and wife at home or while attending activities with them. A reality Jeff said his wife would routinely point out. Then there was Shubhi, starting her 13th year at work. She shared a routine I heard from many. She went to work each day, did what she needed to do, and classified her time at work filled mostly with the stress, suck or saga routine. But Shubhi reassured me all was well. Noting to me several times in our conversations it was all worth it. For one day someday she would get all that she wanted. Shubhi was in a situation some have called the golden handcuffs.

None of this is wrong and none of this is right. Our life grows numb inside the walls of The Work-Life Escape Room, from the reality created by how we spend most of the time at work. Consequently, we lose the ability to see we are not our best selves most of the time, most days each week. Without realizing it, we grow comfortable with the familiar sights and sounds of the stress, suck, or saga routine. Just like we do with the smog, smell and sounds as we routinely sit in roadway traffic. My intent is not to be negative or harsh. I believe you are more than you find yourself in the present day, and so do you. But you're surrounded by noise that tells you to keep doing more the same. This is how The Work-life Escape Room wants you to play the remaining time in your work-life.

It took me breaking and it shouldn't have. We need to stop "shoulding all over our lives." I shouldn't have had to break before saying, *"Hey, wait a minute…I am not living most of my waking life in time that brings me what I really want."* Instead, I was breathing all the normalized dysfunction caught up in the business, noise, and distraction of being a job. And I was successful. But I, like you and others, had to make a choice. It was not easy to choose to move so I could breathe and be who I wanted and live a work-life where I could get what I really wanted most of the time. Nor was it easy living a work-life being who the job told me to be. You may have heard of this question: *"What would you say if you could tell your younger self one thing?"* I'd first reflect that riding in all the first-class seats, having the money, and travelling all over the world was fantastic until you realize what all that can cost. I would then discuss how I embodied working hard, ensured work got done before all else, and hustled for the job first. Hard work, dedication, and commitment are all important things. But I was working hard, being dedicated, and committed to living a work-life where I was not getting what I really wanted most of the time. What authentically I held deep inside. Yet more the same I remained. This meant I missed thousands of hours with my family, I missed thousands of hours enjoying time with friends, and I missed thousands of hours of living life as the best me. Consequently, the people, places, and things I cared for most also missed out. Shame on me for that. I lived with that guilt for a long time. And then I realized across all these people I had talked with for all these years, it was so much the same thing. We were all trapped in The Work-life Escape Room. So, what is the one thing I would say to my younger self?

> *Champions play the game differently, so dare to spend most of the time in your waking life authentically for what you really want and dare to breathe and be the person you believe is impossible to be.*

Before I leave you with your first major choice, I want to pass on one last perspective. An old friend once told me, *"Everyone is faking it; some are just better at it than others."* Who do you want to be while you play the game of work-life? Like the many around or who you authentically want to breathe and be? What stands in our way is not our inability, rather it is our choice of who we choose to be. The current work-life is full of distractions and noise. And in it, little space exists to see there is another choice. The code that brought many of us into work-life taught us to play the game with routines more the same. And in these routines, there is no space to breathe and be the person we really want to be. So, we set that person aside and lock it up in place it can hide. We then lived a significant portion of our lives in our own race against time. In time we can't say we have wanted or loved living in most of the time. We played by the rules that said work hard today and tomorrow is yours. But arriving to tomorrow can never be certain. This makes the value you, me and many get out of today more concerning. Are you getting what you want in return from the time you spend most of your waking life? Or are you betting on the chance of tomorrow? I, too, have friends and family that have made that bet, and some have cashed in. But when we look at what they got it is interesting to think about the cost. Many spent 30 or 40 years to get 10 or 20. This Misdirection has taught us to play the game of work-life by spending dollars to get dimes. But this, of course, only comes from what value any of us place on our time. What that value is for you is for you to decide.

You know there is a person inside you really want to be but are not living. You are not living that person because that person is trapped. You put that person in a box, put that box in a back room, turned off the light, closed the door and locked it. The good news is this version of you still exists, but it's locked away. Constrained by society, friends, and family who have said you can't do that, you have to do this, think this way, and be someone else. And if you wonder why you might feel tired or burned out as you live in your current work-life, my friend Blue might call this a clue. And if you feel all of this should be easy, it's not. So please give yourself a break. You are where you are because you did nothing wrong. You have worked hard and did what you were told. None of this is about what is right or what's wrong. This is about choosing what you want in most of your waking life.

I have done my best to express and expose the backdrop of this game - a game where many of us have been trapped most of our waking lives. I would love for you not to have to 'should' all over your life. But what you do now is entirely up to you and not for any others to choose. Where you are is where this starts. Choose to stay and be more the same or choose to move and escape The Work-life Escape Room.

The Chamber of Cerberus

"I dare you to move." —Jon and Tim Foreman

The reality many describe most times in their work-life is one that often feels hard, boring, or sometimes cold and hurtful. And because of that, the idea of feeling tired or exhausted most of the time, most days of the week, instead of energized and vitalized continues to be expected and rationalized. Please don't take my word for it as the great Levar Burton might subscribe. Think back to conversations you have had at a diner, a bar, or at a gathering where you talked about time at work with friends or family. How often have stories been shared describing someone feeling enslaved or exhausted from working hour after hour doing things they felt had no real meaning, purpose, or impact other than paying bills or living another day just to make another dollar? Did other stories shared describe situations of time spent at work as if the person telling the story felt they were in chains or had to face madness or monsters? And what about stories I have felt or heard all too often? Stories shared where time at work felt like there was no place for anyone to express their true face or a place for their true voice to be heard. Instead of being the person someone wanted to be and knew could make a difference, they conceded and worked hard to be who they weren't. Or the ever-popular reality where time spent at work is often found working for a boss who is condescending and doesn't care about anything more than what justifies their own positioning and agenda. And the list can go on and on. What about you? Can you think of stories you shared of your own work-life or heard from others? Is it fair to assume many described most of the time they have lived their life at work was in the stress, suck or saga routine? Or in a place where they felt unhappy, uninspired, or unfulfilled most of the time, most days each week?

What about when someone shared an idea describing a different work-life? A work-life no one in the room currently had? As the stories unfolded didn't a different kind of energy filled the room. One where a hope of happiness, inspiration or fulfillment could be considered. And if these moments occurred while at a restaurant, bar, or gathering with family or friends, didn't you happen to see this new energy expressed further while people scribbled on napkins? But then the clock struck 12, and poof, it was over. The friends or family you were talking with left, and the time you had that day was gone. Then the next day arose, and more of the same. You found yourself again living with the rationalized dissatisfaction as you lived most of the time in the new day living back in a work-life more the same.

Suppose we could pause briefly here a moment and reflect. Wouldn't it be fair to suggest the descriptions of most stories shared by you, friends, or your family could be easily mistaken for some of Stephen's King's remarkable work? But the stories shared are not fictional. Their origin not from books or movies. These are the stories of real lives trapped in a twisted, tortuous, and tangled game.

Welcome to The Work-Life Escape Room.

An obvious place where many constantly complain yet choose to stay and continue to do more of the same. A place many including you have lived in for so long it's oblivious there is any other place to play the work-life game. Whether you escape from it, or it keeps you trapped in it for the remainder of your work-life will come down to what you decide to do. Choose to stay or choose to move.

In front of you is a door. A door you entered some time ago because of many things you were once told. Get the money, put in the most time, and earn the titles and promotions that come to those who hustle and grind. These are the things constantly told to me, you and many all around. And are the things measured to determine who's who in the crowd. Things so large in our life they become what we mostly see. Things that prevent us from seeing work-life differently. If you want something different than more of the same, you will have to find a way to escape. But you can't leave from the door you entered because the first obstacle standing in your way.

Welcome to Obstacle #1
A Three-Headed Dog Named Cerberus

Cerberus is a massive beast. A beast we live most our work-life staring at most days each week. A beast of the money, the time, and the hustle and grind. A beast so large we can't move him out of our way. Instead dare you must choose to move and look at work-life in a completely new way. From this point forward should you ever choose to stay on any day until the day you escape you will return back to Cerberus. And if you do, every time that occurs, you will be presented with the same choice. Choose to stay and remain more the same or choose to move and dare to escape.

THE BEAST THAT KEEPS US WITHIN

FROM THE DOOR YOU ENTERED, AWAKE AND WARM,
A PLACE SAID TO YOU SINCE YOU WERE BORN,
YOU HAVE SPENT CONSIDERABLE EFFORT, MONEY, AND TIME,
TO GET THE BENEFITS OF BEING INSIDE,
AND IF YOU BELIEVE THE GAME MUST BE WON,
SPEND MORE YOU HAVE TO GET THE JOB DONE,
YET EACH DAY, YOU LOOK, AS YOU WALK AROUND,
FOR PIECES OF YOU THAT WILL NEVER BE FOUND,
THE BEST OF YOU DOESN'T LIVE TODAY,
CONDITIONED TO COMPARE, BE MORE THE SAME,
BUT TO THINK THERE IS MORE THAN YOU FIND TODAY,
IS CONFUSING TO THE COMFORT IN THE DAY THAT'S BEEN
MADE,
IN THE END, YOU MAY, AS OTHERS BEFORE,
GET WHAT COMES FROM ENTERING THE SAME DOOR,
BUT TODAY IS NOT TOMORROW AND IS ALL YOU GET,
FACED WITH A DILEMMA OF WHERE LIFE'S SPENT,
AND IF YOU DARE DECIDE YOU WANT MORE,
FIND YOU MUST A HIDDEN DOOR,
BUT STANDING TALL AND BLOCKING YOUR WAY,
A THREE HEADED DOG FORCED TO STAY,
SO TURN YOU MUST FROM COMFORT OR FEAR,
FACE THE DIRECTION OF WHAT YOU HOLD DEAR,
DO WHAT YOU WANT; IT'S UP TO YOU,
CHOOSE TO STAY OR CHOOSE TO MOVE.

If you choose to look at work-life in a new way, you must be willing to turn around in a direction most never look. This means you will have to choose to be like a ship leaving the harbor. You will have to look away from the comfort and familiarity of what you know and what those around you expect and routinely holler. You must be willing to look into the dark, embrace the cold, and face a journey that will only grow harder. Knowing if you do you will be ridiculed by those you may feel are your biggest supporters.

Welcome to Choice #1—The Choice to Stay or Move

Choosing to move is first a choice to turn away from Cerberus. This is not an easy thing to do. In fact, in reflection of myself and hundreds before you, this choice is one of the hardest in the room. But remember:

Rule #3   Where you look is where you can choose to move and go.

So if more than a good enough work-life is what you want, choosing to turn is the choice you must make.

CHOOSE TO STAY OR CHOOSE TO MOVE

IF NO LONGER YOU ACCEPT WHAT YOU SEE WITH YOUR EYES,
WHAT SEEMS AS TRUTH, BUT YOU KNOW IS LIES,
IT'S TIME TO TURN TO WHAT YOU CAN'T SEE,
KNOWING MANY WILL NOT WANT YOU TO LEAVE,
IF MORE YOU WANT THAN WHAT COMMON IS FOUND,
DARE YOU MUST TURN AWAY FROM THE CROWD,
FIND YOUR WAY OUT THE ESCAPE ROOM DOOR,
INTO A DAY UNIQUELY YOURS,
THE TIME IN YOUR LIFE IS ALL YOU GET,
SPEND IT GETTING WHAT YOU WANT OR SPEND IT ON REGRET,
WHAT YOU DO IS UP TO YOU,
CHOOSE TO STAY OR CHOOSE TO MOVE.

The choice to turn is not a choice without resistance. To help you see this resistance before you face it, let me share with you some insight from Sierra and Tom. Sierra shared that the decision to move was the scariest thing she had ever decided to do. She had found most of her work-life was full of discomfort, but bills got paid, and seeing how to do it any other way was something she couldn't see how to do. But one day, after three months of pondering in her mind and talking to her therapist, she told herself she had to do something different. On that day she decided to turn. When she did, she almost immediately froze and felt as if she couldn't move. It's one thing to tell yourself you are ready for a change, and it is another to act on what you say. During our conversation, we discovered the journey up to this point was similar to waiting in line for the newest roller coaster at a local amusement park. You know, the one advertised as the fastest, with the biggest loops, drops, and craziest upside-down flips. Before getting on, you're laughing with your friends, seeing others having a good time. But then it's your turn. The attendant locks you in and wishes you a fun ride. Suddenly, it's just you in the seat, and things feel different. You close your eyes, trying to escape the reality of what's about to happen. It's the reality you chose, but now it feels scary. On the other side of this experience is Tom. Tom's response to putting himself into the new scary roller coaster was one that said, *"Let's go."* While sharing his story with me, Tom routinely expressed his desire for growth and the ability to see new things. This was evident when I started speaking with Tom. He was mid-way through his seventh job in less than ten years. My story resonates more with Tom's approach because an important thing I really want in most of my work-life is adventure. But guess what happened to Tom and me when we decided we would turn? We both froze, just like Sierra and many in the hundreds I spoke with over those twelve years. Why did this happen? Because rarely have any of us looked at work-life in any other way except for staring at Cerberus. So, a choice like that is unfamiliar. And as such, can be scary.

Equally difficult for some before was recognizing the choice alone is not all that is required. Choosing to turn away from Cerberus means you must also move.

To help you do this, here is the summary of steps that have helped many of us before:

1. Go to a mirror in your house or find one you can hold in your hand.

2. Now, look at yourself and think about what you want most from the time in your waking life.

As you may soon recognize, there is a good chance you will find yourself, like many of us before, unable to say or see yourself having what you really want most of the time. Things you hold authentically true deep inside that find you happy, inspired, or fulfilled. The good news is at this stage of the game, all you need to do is turn, and you can do this without being able to see or say any of this. Remember...

Rule #4   If you don't write it down and say it out loud,
whatever it is will never come true.

3. Write down or say to yourself "The time of my life is worth more to me than what I am spending it on in my current work-life."

Like a security system you might find in your house or existing in some business, when The Work-Life Escape Room detects something not the same, the room will be alerted. This means as you start to move and turn in a new direction you will hear sounds and noises from society, friends, and family. You will also find coordinated distractions will be placed in front of you everywhere you look. Up, down, and all around. You will hear sounds and noises telling you, *"There is no way." "How would you do this thing that you want?" "You have bills to pay and responsibilities to handle." "The idea may be amazing, but the reality of it is impossible." "It's too risky." "You have already put in too much time to leave."* And because at this stage of the game, you will be unable to see how you can have this different work-life reality, you will be vulnerable to believing these sounds and noises. Over and over, these sounds and noises from society, friends, and family will echo in your mind. They are dangerous because they attack you on the inside. And to make matters worse, these sounds and noises are not the only thing coming your way. Why has choice #1 been viewed as one of the hardest in the room? Because accomplishing the turn means facing two obstacles at once.

THE MADNESS OF MEDIOCRITY

OBVIOUS, OBLIVIOUS, AND ALL AROUND,
A CONVINCING TRUTH HAS DIRECTED OUR HEADS DOWN,
AND THROUGH OUR EYES, WHAT CAN'T WE SEE,
EVERYTHING YOU, I, AND EVERYONE COULD BE,
ITS WHISPERS ARE GENTLE, ITS APPEARANCE IS WARM,
AND AMONGST US ALL, EACH DAY IT IS BORN,
ITS POWER SO GREAT, OH HOW I WISH YOU COULD SEE,
WITHOUT EVER TOUCHING, IT CONSTRAINS US TO BE,
WHAT IT IS, WHAT IT ISN'T, IS ITS EXPRESSIVE CURSE,
AND EVERY DAY, IT SITS AMONGST US WITH A READIED HEARSE,
FOR WHAT IT DOES IS NOTHING BUT CONVINCE US TO BE,
NOTHING MORE THAN MEDIOCRITY.

Welcome to Obstacle #2
The Madness of Mediocrity

The Madness of Mediocrity is impossible to ignore. And worse yet, it likely exists at least partially in many things you adore. Because this madness is impossible to ignore, you must face it by creating another sound. A sound from a source buried deep, locked up, and hidden far away. This sound is something called your whisper. While the idea of this may sound silly, no pun intended, your whisper is the expression where your authentic dreams and unique perspectives are born. It is an expression that is necessary to discover all the things that would make up your ideal work-life.

The challenge to discover my whisper was not common because for me it was harder than the turn from Cerberus. The challenge I faced represented the self-described disorder I have felt my entire life. As I wrote in the book Game On - Leaders Who Last, my whisper represented the literal expression of my voice. A voice that was often very different from others and was the reason I told myself I hated the way I thought, talked, and saw the world. A difference that was commonly critiqued by society, friends, and family through sounds and noises suggesting to me my voice was disruptive and not desired. This restrained the expression of my authentic dreams and unique perspectives for years. Looking across my career there were cluses where my whisper tried to come out. But because it wasn't popular in what society, friends, and family echoed every day, it would constantly be critiqued and constrained. For years, I played my game of work-life in a place that beat my whisper down. It started when I was learning the code from my earliest days as a child. At a time when my whisper came out, but when it did, it was screamed at by my biological father. Then, after I entered work-life, I found myself in positions where, at times, I felt safe to try and let my whisper come again. Yet only to find it ridiculed and told over and over again to put it away, get in line and be more the same just like others playing the same work-life game. As I began to promote myself, I saw similar experiences in the people I led. When I would bring this observation up to colleagues and other leaders, we all worked for, I heard over and over again instructions telling me that was not what needed to be focused on, that's not a real issue. As I moved even higher and put myself in the C-Suit, I saw the perspectives from business owners, board members, and executive colleagues. Perspectives that frequently viewed people below them as second class. May I also dare to share a perspective that still makes me sick to my stomach to think about. A perspective where an owner of a company I worked at for years truly saw his employees as subservient handouts. A point he would communicate behind closed doors when expressing position and authority with others. These experiences reinforced a belief it was better to get in line, do what I was told and be more the same. As a result, I buried my authentic dreams and unique perspectives under layers of frustration, fear, and comfort just like many of the people I spoke with. Like my whisper and many others, there is a good chance your whisper is hidden underneath years of fear, comfort, or frustration. Be aware this also means to go get your whisper you will have to explore memories or circumstances connected to one, some, or all that fear, comfort, or frustration in order to find it.

Finding your whisper and other things you will need to find to escape The Work-Life Escape Room will require you look for and find clues. Finding clues to help you find your whisper starts by:

1. Think about a time in your life you can say with no hesitation you were happy, inspired or fulfilled.

2. Now, think a little deeper about that time. What about that time was authentic to what you really want deep inside?

3. Now think about a time when you were just being you? No, not the made-up you that you have played as much of your work-life, the real you.

4. Think about what it meant to be the real you. During that time didn't you feel free and alive? Living in a time of your life that felt light, fun, and effortless.

5. Now think about what words might have described the things you want found during the time you were happy, inspired or fulfilled.

6. Now, begin to think about how you could phrase a string of words that describes the essence of all the things you just thought about. A phrase you can write down, say, and remember.

At this stage of the game, it's important not to forget:

Rule #3   Where you look is where you can choose to move and go.

And be aware the common tactic used by The Madness of Mediocrity is to amplify the sounds and noises of your most vulnerable distraction. For me, the madness ensured I kept seeing the status, perks, and promotions I was leaving. When I was able to fight that off, it would strike me in the gut and ask me how I was going to pay my bills or be able to respond to any sickness or commotion. And the more I would dare to continue to find my whisper, the louder, more alluring, and concerning the madness would fight me each day. If I, you, or others can't find our whisper, the ability to move in the direction of an ideal work-life stops.

Like me, through focus and determination you too will eventually find your whisper. Please keep in mind for many including me it may take some considerable time. Why? Because there is a good chance your whisper is weak from all the years of being ignored and malnourished. Efforts to create conditions where focused and uninterruptable time can be spent have been found productive for many to find their whisper. For some, that has meant going into a dark room, putting their hands physically over their ears, closing their eyes, and just sitting as they start their day. For others like me, it was a space placed in each evening as I prepared for the oncoming day. Whatever works for you is fine to do. It's more about having a consistent focus to find your whisper until you do. Once you hear it, there is a good chance it may sound weird. Some have said when they first heard their whisper, it sounded bonkers but true. Others described it as calmly incoherent. It doesn't matter how wacky, weird, or out of this world your whisper may appear. You whisper is your whisper, and it gets to be whatever it wants to be. I wish I could tell you something more prescriptive than that. But it has always been the case for everyone thus far; once they heard it, they knew it. It may not make sense, but to you, your whisper will make total sense. And don't be embarrassed when you find your whisper. I am confident that you are most likely the only one in the world who will fully get it. And that is okay. Your whisper is authentic to you and no one else. Not your kids, spouse, partner, best friend, mom, neighbor, boss, cousin, or any other human. But please know that I can almost guarantee with absolute certainty you will see the madness seeking to convince you otherwise. If you were curious about what mine was and still is, let me share it.

Do you, be Dave's Disorder.

A phrase rarely understandable or relatable to anyone else. Mine represents the voice I was never allowed to bring to the world or always had to defend when trying.

Over the years, there have been many ways to describe how the whisper can appear once it can be heard. Most commonly, they have been thought of in three ways. The most popular has been to think about it as a champion chant—the message used to arrive and win the big championship. Similar to what you may see in a sports team. Another common way has been to think of it like people campaigning for some position. Those who have thought of it that way call it the campaign message. And a lesser but still popular way you whisper might appear could be relatable if you are someone who has played video games before. When thought of in the context of a video game, the whisper has been described as a "Power Up". No matter what you want to call it, your whisper is the one message that is just a few words like mine or could be said with many sentences. Words that can be thought about, written down or said that will help you move through the dark, embrace the cold, and face challenges and monsters untold.

Over the years, there have been some fascinating stories about people finding their whispers; while you continue to work on finding yours, let me share a few others with you. Years back, I met with Jesus, who taught English as a second language. Jesus came up with his phrase, *"I am gifted, fast, and fearless."* And then there was Susan, who decided her phrase was *"I am a knitting heart."* That confused me even more. You see, at the time, Susan was in charge at a local Department of Motor Vehicles (DMV) site. For those who might need clarification of what that is. It is the place many of us visit to get or renew our driver's licenses. When Jesus escaped The Work-Life Escape Room, he didn't arrive at a work-life that found him as a professional race car driver he always dreamed of. But he did arrive at one where he became semi-pro. Susan spent fourteen years at the DMV, a place she openly stated she hated. But she did so for all the right reasons. The day Susan ultimately escaped, she found herself helping make families and communities she never had. This meant a lot to Susan because she grew up with a family heavily into drugs, with a father who would assault her routinely, and found herself every year or two arriving to a new place she had to call home. Now, Susan was running a group connecting kids who faced similar days with parents who loved them in ways she never got to taste. I remember chatting with her about a year after she escaped, and before saying a word, the light in her eyes told me everything was ok. *"More than okay"* was what Susan expressed as she shared all the things she was doing. She also shared how she felt free in the time she spent at work. Time that allowed her to no longer carry the weight and pain of her childhood.

Something interesting occurred uniquely special, yet more the same, in all those who before escaped. More times than not, three things have been found—time spent in work-life was no longer in the stress, suck or saga routine most days of the week, bills were getting paid, and people said they were having fun most of the time.

It is often exciting to find your whisper and bring it into the day enough to help you turn away from Cerberus and drown out some of the sound and noises from the madness. An experience energized as you complete the turn and see a new door. One you have never seen before. But then, as suddenly as the swells of excitement appeared, they will be gone. For many, as it was for me, and it is anticipated that it will be for you, is the realization of a new kind of pressure. Caused by something that has been wrapped around your ankle since the beginning of your work-life. Chains that have attached you to expectations and all the things that said,

Go be a job.

Welcome to Obstacle #3
The Chains of Our Restraint

The chains are what keep you connected to all the things you find familiar. In a twisted way, you, me and many have worn the chains for so long we have grown comfortable with them on. A comfort so familiar it was not uncommon to see some before becoming fearfully uncomfortable when they took them off, so they almost immediately put their chains back on. As you face obstacle #3, the madness will focus on distracting you. The madness will continue its charge to tell you things like *"You are not," "You can't be,"* and *"Things are better if you just stay where you are."* When you don't listen to what the madness has to say, don't be surprised to hear its sounds and noises becoming louder and more obnoxious day after day. Mixing in the unique way that will start to get in your way. Making whatever sound or noises are necessary to convince you to stay. For Mason and Susan, it began to attack them in a very vulnerable way. Telling them if they took of the chains, they would *"not be able to take care of their kids in the proper way."* The worst they shared was when the madness used their friends and family to encourage them to stay and constantly tried to convince them staying was safer and more supported.

In all the years, I have rarely seen those who completed the turn away from Cerberus lack the desire to remove the chains. And yet, almost all, including me, struggled to remove them. So, let me be clear. At this stage of the game, it is okay if you feel what you must do is hard. Removing the Chains of Our Restraint is not an easy thing to do. The chains are heavy with everything familiar. They are secured by a lock when it's touched, causes the room to respond and begin echoing back the beliefs you have told yourself for a very long time. These beliefs are the scripts you have said all these years. Scripts full of repeated and rationalized reasons why you have stayed in the room. These scripts will tell you taking the chains off is selfish and wrong. And if you do, the people, places, and things you care for most will all be gone. Worst yet, at this stage of the room, you are still in the dark. It's cold, and you cannot see where you are. You are also surrounded by society, friends, and family, telling you it's irresponsible to remove the chains, so staying where you are is best.

For me, taking off the chains felt like I was not doing what was needed for everyone else. Once I did, I agonized about it for days and months, routinely filled with fear. This may be an area you and I largely have in common. For much of our adult life, and for the right reasons, we have focused to ensure things were in order for the people, places, and things we care for most. Yet to be our best self, for others and ourselves, we must take off the chains. The Chains of our Restraint are secured by a coded lock designed to remain shut and keep you from moving where you are. The good news is you can find this code while being in the dark.

Here are the steps to unlock the lock:

1. Believe in your whisper, the one you may feel is true inside, knowing you will most likely be unable to see how it can be a lived reality for you most of the time.

2. Make a bet on that belief.

3. Commit to your bet on that belief even though you cannot see how getting it is possible.

If you do these three things, the lock will open.

The challenge with the Chains of our Restraint is that we have to remove it and continue resisting the sounds and noises that tell us to put it back on. A similar analogy is the everyday struggle of losing and keeping off body weight. Like losing body weight, the chains are not something you take off, and then it's done. Once you take them off, you can put them right back on. I won't be rude and call you out; I will call myself out. I, in fact, put the chains back on several times in my journey out of The Work-Life Escape Room. Like eating food full of too many calories, I fell back many times into the comfortable routines of doing more of the same. Living my work-life most days with the stress, suck, or saga routine. And each time I did, I found myself back at the start of the game. Standing near Cerberus and the chants from society, friends, and family, all of whom were playing the counting game.

I will tell you I wanted to take the chains off badly. Because I wanted to stop feeling like I was "dying in the building." But, just like losing weight, wanting to take the chains off isn't enough. If you want to move toward the new door you see, you must take off the chains and keep them off for the remainder of your work life. It may feel impossible, but you are already everything you need to be.

YOU ALREADY ARE

YOU ARE MORE THAN YOU ALLOW,
IT'S TIME NOW TO LEAVE THE CROWD,
A GIFT UNIQUE THAT NEEDS TO BREATHE,
BELIEVE IN YOU, BECOME YOUR BELIEF,
BUT MORE THAN BELIEF IS REQUIRED,
FOR WHAT YOU WANT AND DESIRE,
IN LIES YOU, THE KEY YOU NEED,
TO BET AND COMMIT TO WHAT YOU COULD BE,
SO MAKE TODAY THE DAY YOU MADE,
AND DECIDE FOR YOURSELF TO MOVE AWAY,
RELEASE YOURSELF FROM THE CHAINS,
THAT'S KEPT YOU SILENT TO THE PAIN,
IT'S TIME NOW TO BE THE PERSON INSIDE,
AND UNBOX ALL THE PIECES YOU HIDE,
THE JOURNEY TO BECOMING YOUR BEST SELF,
BEGINS THE DAY, YOU UNLOCK YOURSELF.

I wish I could tell you this is all it took for me and many before to remove the chains and keep them off. Like you now, we too had the information we needed. Information that told us how to take the chains off and keep them off. Yet, having this information didn't make what we needed to do easy. Similar to the resistance you may have felt as you started to turn away from Cerberus, removing the chains requires more than intention and courage. So, if you find yourself struggling, let me share with you a source of energy that may help you. An energy that has helped many before, like you, remove the chains. This source is something you can think of as "the time of no".

Upfront, I do need to tell you this source may or may not be available to you. Like many things in the room, what you are presented as options has a lot to do with the state by which you are ready to escape. To help you look for clues, let me briefly tell you about Nathan and Chad. Nathan knew he was better than who he was living in his current work-life. But day after day, he continued to endure a good enough work-life because it provided the things he needed for his family. Back and forth, week after week and month after month, he danced in his mind about what to do. Nathan shared that his current boss, Ramon, not only treated him horribly most of the time, he treated many others the same. He intentionally used and stepped on top of them for the sole purpose of seeking his promotion. Nathan described his boss, and I quote, *"In his short fat stature was the biggest egoistical *Dave Edit— not a nice word."* Nathan felt exhausted and drained most of the time in his work-life from the enduring onslaught of passive-aggressive assaults he and his colleagues routinely received. But Nathan had the job he worked years to get. The money and the benefits were great, and he was afraid there was no way to maintain his achievements. So, each day, he put up with the mouth of Ramon and came home most nights very tired and worn.

Chad, on the other hand, from years of hard work and hustle, finally got the promotion to lead the team he always wanted. The first year was filled with fun and discovery, but then, a few months into his second year, something happened. Chad was now overseeing 15 people. Drawing from his experience the previous year, he believed he had the insights necessary to bring about meaningful changes – changes he thought would benefit everyone involved. By 'everyone,' Chad meant his team, himself, his boss, and the company. All he needed was approval from his boss.

On the day of the meeting, he dressed sharply, wearing a new shirt with cufflinks his wife had given him a year prior to celebrate his promotion. Confident his presentation had all the answers to the questions his boss would have, Chad entered his boss's office, believing his ideas would be well-received.

His presentation was organized in a way he knew his boss liked to review material. It praised his boss's accomplishments and proposed changes that would align and further promote them. As Chad reminisced, he seemed almost to suspend the turning world as he returned to those moments. It was a time when he felt energized, alive, and excited to bring his boss ideas on how time spent at work could be better for all.

At first, Chad's boss read the contents of his presentation slowly, as if being careful not to miss any word. And then, as if there was a newfound urgency, Chad shared how his boss began flipping through his presentation quickly, at a pace where the content on any given page could, at best, be scanned. I am unsure I will ever forget how Chad's face and tone changed when he told me what happened next and the answer he received. It was as if the previous moments in the story were a fully blown-up balloon of excitement, instantly gone when he was told his proposal was not approved, justified by the piercing phrase, "This is not how we do things here.

Years would pass before I would unexpectedly hear from Nathan or Chad again. Nathan reached out first and said, *"Hi, Dave, I can't do it anymore."* About nine or so months after hearing from Nathan,

Chad reached out and shared that he had followed everything his boss told him, was now at an even higher level in the hierarchy and was tired of how he felt most of the time in his work-life. Said in his words, *"I am done with this; my life is too short to continue to live this way."*

Some have been able to take off their chains and keep them off on the very first try. Many, including me, Nathan, and Chad, did not. It took us several tries. Each time we tried, we faced rule #5.

Rule #5   You can never go back or forward the same way you came

Eventually we found the clues we needed. Clues that allowed us to find the "time of no" and use it. Your work-life may not yet be in a state where its deterioration has gone so far while trapped in the room that the "time of no" is available. But if it is, knowing about this hidden source of energy is helpful in aiding your escape.

Freeing from the chains with the conviction to take them off and keep them off is a gift. But if you are not careful, it can be a curse. You see, as soon as you take off the chains, you can move in ways you have never moved before. But like with any movement, if you move wrong, you can get hurt. In my own experience, and those commonly shared, the act of taking off the chains can bring on an overwhelming sense of relief and release. And in that moment, an excitement to move as quickly as possible. Dare I say for some, that even meant having a feeling to run. The problem is at this stage of The Work-life Escape Room the chamber is still so dark you cannot yet see, and the air is filled with toxicity from the madness. This means before moving toward the new door, you must first learn how to breathe and move in a different way than you have before.

Our ability to breathe is critical to how we move and how we use our head, heart, and hands in our work-life. This is why you can now expect the room to use the madness and society, friends, and family with an increased focus to convince you to keep breathing the same. If they are successful, you will not escape.

In all the stories, there was a glaring commonality found across mine and many. A commonality I believe you also may share. An authentic vulnerability and committed desire to breathe most of the time, most days each week focused first on doing whatever it takes to see the people, places, and things cared for most have what they need. Many of us have lived with this committed concern for so long its presence is comfortable. Living our work-lives most days each week focused on putting others first. Even when that meant sacrificing some aspect of being happy, inspired, or fulfilled in our work-life. On the surface any critique for having a committed concern for putting others first may sound inappropriate. With respect for those right reasons and our other connected concern to see you escape, let's briefly discuss a time you rode in an airplane.

You and I have never been on the same commercial airplane at the same time (at least that we know of). And yet, no matter who you, me, or any of us are, where we live, or what we do, every time we have flown in a commercial airplane, we have heard one specific instruction about breathing. *"Put your mask on first before helping others."* Yet, beyond the plane we forget this important rule. We condition and over time grow accustomed to think sacrificing the best of our time as something to praise, promote, and sometimes defend. Haven't you seen your parents, or someone you knew, or even yourself go and say, *"I have to sacrifice for… fill in the blank." Statements like these are often made with the right reasons and good intentions in mind. However, what if, instead of making sacrifices, we intentionally focused on activities that enable us to act on our good intentions while being and breathing our best?* How much better could we show up and support the people, places and things we care about most. To put it differently, we may function adequately when we show up as our 80% selves, but operating at 80% is not being our best.

To escape The Work-life Escape Room, you will need to learn to breathe through your whisper. Hearing this may sound silly and simple. Yet, nothing can be further from the truth. Breathing through your whisper means breathing most of the time in work-life with what your whisper says. This means there will be several things you will need to learn to tell no or simply ignore.

Knowing how to breathe is only half of the equation. You must also learn to move in a new way. The most common setback at this stage of the room has been caused by a desire to move too quickly. Instead, you must learn how to move forward in a way you can think of as "inward and inches." The word inward ensures your movement is connected to your whisper. And the word inches allow you to move under increasingly hard resistance. Some have expanded the translation further, saying, *"You must move in inches; not feet or centimeters, not meters."* Translate it however you like, but the literal sense is required. You must breathe your whisper into how you think and what you expect from your work-life. You must also understand the biggest progress is made from small steps at a time.

There is more to moving under the focus and expectation of inward and inches that has often been overlooked. In lived reality, making effort every day to escape The Work-Life Escape Room doesn't mean you will move forward. In fact, there will be days every week I can confidently guarantee you will find yourself moving backward. There has never been a person moving through the room who has not had a "backward day." But this isn't a problem if you learn to move with "inward and inches" movement. Why this has been found to be productive to the effort of escaping the room is because inward keeps you pointed toward the new door and an inch per day is an achievable distance. This creates movement that is smooth, like the tortoise race against the hare. And smooth is fast. This also means each week you can have up to three backward days and still be closer to the new door than you were a week before. It is also important for you to know a hidden truth was discovered in this part of the game. One that allows you to turn a "backward day" to your advantage. The truth is, when you find yourself in a "backward day" no matter how hard you try, nothing is going to go your way. This makes recognizing when they arrive straightforward. Instead of fighting with them and holding on tightly to expectations, you can use the time in a "backward day" for rest and recovery.

The first time you try and move using "inward and inches" movement you will most likely feel clumsy. But little by little, you will begin to get your stride. And once you do, you will find you have arrived. In front of you stands the new door. The one you have wanted to reach since you first turned from Cerberus. And this is the door to escape his Chamber. True to being in an escape room, you will find this door is locked. To unlock it you must solve a puzzle.

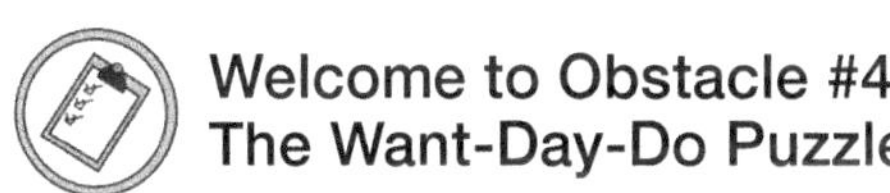

Welcome to Obstacle #4
The Want-Day-Do Puzzle

This puzzle is presented to deceive you into thinking it is easy to solve. But I beg you not to fall for this trap. To date, I have yet to meet anyone who has solved this puzzle with ease, including me. This puzzle must be solved using your whisper in an unobstructed way. A huge problem that has been found is quieting the madness existing all around. Because the madness cannot be completely ignored, you will need a way to deal with it in order to solve this puzzle.

The good news is a way has been found. This way is by using something called the "Jar of Work-Life Struggle."

Steps to use the Jar of Work-Life Struggle.

1. Imagine a jar or, better yet, as some have done, go and get some type of physical jar.

2. Next, write out any and all work-life struggles on anything that can capture your writing and be put in the jar. It has been common to see people use paper, sticky pads, and napkins.

3. Finally, place the jar away from you at a distance of your choosing. Some have preferred to put it in another room, while others have kept it right next to them.

Knowing your work-life struggles are accounted for will allow you to temporarily pause, breathe deeply and listen to your whisper as you work to solve obstacle #4. Don't worry, your work-life struggles are not going anywhere. They are right there in your jar. Available to you, whenever you want to go back to them.

It's now time for you to face obstacle #4. An obstacle that helps you answer what you couldn't clearly before.

Describe what you want in your ideal work-life.

This means describing all the things you really want most of the time while you live your life at work. The things meaningfully connected, purposeful, and impactful to what you hold authentically true deep inside.

To complete. the Want-Day-Do puzzle, use the worksheet made available or a blank sheet of paper, space on a tablet or other writing surface, and complete the following:

1. Write everything you want from your ideal work-life. As you do, please remember:

Rule #4 :   If you don't write it down and say it out loud, whatever it is will never become in your lived reality.

There is a good chance you will struggle writing this list to its full potential. This struggle is caused by the sounds and the noises still echoing all around. Telling you that you can't have what you really want or the things you write down are wrong. Don't worry about that right now; just write. We will circle back and deal with that issue in another step.

2. Now, on another designated worksheet made available in the book or on a new piece of paper or space on a tablet or other writing surface, describe what your ideal day would look like. And yes, this includes the time before and after any "official" time you spend at work.

3. Finally, on the designated worksheet made available in the book or on a new piece of paper, space on a tablet, or other writing surface, describe what you want to do at work most of the time, most days each week the way you want to do it.

With this complete, let's now address any limitations you have placed in your answer for the Want-Day-Do puzzle.

1. Review your list and highlight anything that is less than "What would you do if nothing was impossible?"

2. Review your list and think about anything you didn't put on it because you couldn't see how to get it. If you discover anything, write it in!

3. For each item in your list, add two additional descriptors to each:

    a. What does each item mean to you? A way this has been productively accomplished was to describe how each item would be explained to someone else.

b. What does each item look like in any given day you would say exist in your ideal work-life?

It may be obvious, and if not, I need to bring it to your attention. From our earliest days in the time before and during school we were taught to regurgitate facts and play by the rules. We all have been conditioned to seek the right answers. Your Want-Day-Do is not about what is right or what is wrong. It's about what is authentically true about what you want most of time you spend at work. You are the only one that can say if this list is true. You can lie to everyone else, but to lie to yourself, yikes! With that said, I must share with you a hidden trap that was found in this part of the game. You can solve the Want-Day-Do puzzle with things that are not authentically true, and the exit door out of The Chamber door will still open. But I promise you will not ultimately be able to escape with a list untrue uniquely to you. So, I beg of you to check back in with yourself. At this stage of the game, all you are doing is writing down what you want in your work-life if nothing were impossible. This included writing things you want, the day you want to have, and the things you want to do on that day the way you want to. You were asked to create an answer using something as authentic to you as the fingerprint on your hand. Your whisper—a phrase that will often seem ridiculous and incoherent to anyone else but you. If you feel your answer to the Want-Day-Do puzzle doesn't seem a little ridiculous or radical, then there might be something still limiting in it. It is important to suggest what the words ridiculous or radical means to you does not have to be the same as anyone else. This means your answer, is your answer. If you go, "This is my answer. It is a little ridiculous or radical, and I don't know how there is any way I am going to get all the things it says in it." Perfect. Now it's done.

You are about to leave The Chamber of Cerberus. It doesn't matter what society, friends, or family wants at this stage of the game. What do you want? This is your opportunity. I don't care if what you want is deemed unacceptable by eight billion and growing. Nor do I care what your kids, spouse, partner, best friend, mom, neighbor, cousins or any other version of a person other than you thinks about what you want, in your ideal work-life. This is your time. If you cannot be selfish here, lets get you back to the start of the game playing with crowds and the counting game.

If you choose to stay, be on your way. I wish you nothing but safe travels back to Cerberus and your current work-life. If you choose to move, please take a moment to breathe and prepare. Because soon you will enter the den of despair also known as The Den of Work-Life Disorder.

THE DAY YOU MADE

COME NOW, THERE IS NOT A MINUTE TO WAIT,
LIFE IS TOO SHORT TO CONTINUE AND HESITATE,
YOU GET TODAY, TOMORROW'S UNTRUE,
SO PLEASE TELL YOURSELF WHAT MATTERS TO YOU,
CHOOSE TO STAY OR CHOOSE TO MOVE.

The Den of Work-Life Disorder

"Don't ask what the world needs; ask what brings you life, and go do that because what the world needs is more people who have come alive." —Howard Thurman

Time lived at work in your head, heart, or hands, regardless of what day or what hour stuck between doing what you feel you must do to survive and doing what you authentically want to thrive alive is the tensional space known as Work-life Disorder. You can see Work-Life Disorder every day in society, and with friends and family. Work-life Disorder often makes people feel unhappy because the disorder muffles and mutes their whispers - the quietest voice inside them that represents the things they authentically want. Consequently, they often feel underrated. Work-life Disorder can also make people feel uninspired because they never arrive where they want to go. With the disorder, people often spread themselves too thin trying to spend their work-life where they feel they must be and where they want to be at the same time. Work-life Disorder can also make people feel unfulfilled because instead of filling themselves up and living most of the time authentically the way they want, it's spent emptying themselves by being who they think they must be.

When someone lives with Work-life Disorder, it can feel like a constant push and pull. For every win, something must be lost. In other words, with Work-life Disorder, life is full of choices between "this or that", with hardly any chances for "this and that." Those of us who have had Work-Life Disorder for any extent of time will tell you most days have some presence of guilt found from sacrificing some aspect of people, places, or things cared for most. Others have said it has felt like a frequent state of anxiousness because they never felt complete. Still others have described it as feeling in a constant state of fatigue–going to bed tired, waking up tired - most days each week.

The Work-Life Disorder stems from the belief time can be manipulated, allowing someone to be in two distinctively different places simultaneously. It was discovered when it was realized authentic work priorities don't exist or are rarely available to the way they are wanted while inside The Work-Life Escape Room. To help you see what was found a little clearer, let me share with you some insights from Lei.

At the time Lei and I spoke, she had just turned 30 a few months prior. She was still in the same job she had held for the past several years prior. Most days, she said she was able to get by, and in the same breath, expressed, *"I just feel uninspired."* Lei shared how she would routinely take things on at work well beyond the position she held or the expectations by which she was hired. She shared how she frequently told people yes more than no because she liked being helpful. It was the feeling of helping she really enjoyed. But in all the effort and energy, Lei shared she never felt she could say she loved most of the time she spent her life at work. This made her feel stuck and frustrated. But Lei didn't accept how she felt so she continued to spend significant time learning everything she could and doing everything she was asked. Yet the conclusion remained more the same. Lei still was not arriving where she wanted to go. In our conversation, Lei would frequently say, *"I can't see and feel blocked no matter what I do."* The answer Lei, I, and others sought wasn't found in the direction of being a job. The struggle arose from our inability to find the time we lived our lives at work with the priorities we each authentically wanted. Priorities that brought us what we really wanted, most of the time, most days each week. We had our whisper, we had our Want-Day-Do, and yet when we tried to bring both into real life, none of us could find our way. Worse yet, the harder we would try the more resistance we would find. And then clues were discovered in the struggle that helped reveal what we once couldn't see. The current work-life said all priorities were the same, yet, each of us had different ones, authentically. A priority on predictability, which in the context of the room, was things such as *"I know when I get paid, repeated work hours mostly the same, an annual raise, and structured responsibilities."* A priority on money, which for most was straightforward. This was a currency of value often thought of as "how much can I get paid?" And, finally, there was a priority of meaning seen as the personal significance someone wants from the time they live their life at work. All of these existed in the current workday, but in the pursuit of being a job, they were mostly implicitly implied, not explicitly considered. Although Lei, I, and many others had these three things on the list of what we wanted from our current work-life, the order in which we had them often was different than what was available. Therefore, like a combination lock, we were never able to unlock time in our work-life in the priority we wanted.

You may have heard someone say, *"You need to get your shit together."* Well, that's what we had to do, and now you do, too.

Welcome to Obstacle #5
The Priority of Our Priorities Puzzle

This puzzle aims to help you gain clarity on your work-life priorities, necessary for unlocking the remaining details of your ideal work-life. This is a puzzle that has been found to be surprisingly refreshing and at the same time uncomforting. On the surface, the energy required to complete this puzzle is much less than the energy required in other faced obstacles. This was refreshing to many of us who arrived at this stage of the game tired and exhausted. Looking at this puzzle deeper may make it a little uncomfortable. Its simple nature highlights such an obvious point many including me were a little embarrassed to have not previously considered. When we have historically went to be a job, three important priorities distinctively different have been conflated. When this conflation occurs, it has been common for someone to want a certain priority but find themselves unable to get it. It has been common for this to occur in one or two ways. The first, is when the priority wanted is missing in the job. In other words, a priority such as meaning may exist in a job, but the authentic way someone wants meaning may not. This might be seen in a teacher who wants meaning from having time that allows them to bring learning and impact to their students yet finds themselves working at a school that views meaning as providing an education focused on numbers in seats and completions. The second common instance found is when a priority exists in a job but not in the order of priorities authentically wanted by a person. An example of this might be when someone mostly wants predictability, but the nature of the job is volatile to certain circumstances. This might be found by people working in sales, where their jobs is predictable as long as they land all the deals.

Realizing there is a work-life priority that is distinctively and authentically more and less important to you is freeing. This allows you to finish describing what you want in your ideal work-life.

The completion of The Priority of our Priorities puzzle will provide you a clear list of your work-life priorities in one of the six variations. They are as follows,

1) predictability first, followed by money, then by meaning, or

2) predictability first, followed by meaning, then by money, or

3) money first, followed by predictability, then by meaning, or

4) money first, followed by meaning than predictability, or

5) meaning first, followed by predictability, then money or

6) meaning first, followed by money, then predictability. *This is my work-life priority

Here are the directions to complete The Priority of our Priorities puzzle:

1. On the designated worksheet made available in the book or on a sheet of paper, space on a tablet, or other writing

surface, you will write out predictability, money, and meaning. And do so in a way where you will have space between each listed priority to place tally numbers or indicate in another way your answer for your Want-Day-Do.

2. Now, associate each item in your Want-Day-Do with one or more categories listed in the Priority of our Priorities puzzle.

Mathematicians may disagree with these rules of logic. But you are not in a math class or at university. You are currently in the Den of Work-Life Disorder. And to get out of it requires doing things differently. As you complete this step, remember two things. First, this is your list, not your kids, spouse, partner, best friend, mom, neighbor, or cousin. Secondly, remember:

Rule #1 & #2 No choice is right or wrong, and fairness is not real. It is either authentic to you, or it is not.

3. Finally, complete a weighting exercise. Count the number of Want-Day-Do items associated with each work-life priority.

For example, I found 33 items from my Want-Day-Do placed in the meaning priority. I had another 11 items placed in the money priority. And finally, I had three items placed in the predictability priority. In my example, my work-life priorities meant I mostly needed to find meaning in the time I spent at work, followed by money, and the lowest of my priorities was predictability. Some have been the same, and others are different.

The point is not what combination you hold. The point is to get your shit together so you can finish getting the code to unlock your ideal work-life. One where most of the time you live your life at work brings you what you really want.

You now have what you need. The details how to describe what your ideal work-life looks like. The priority of what you want from most of the time you live your life at work. What you want to do, how you want to do it. And with this clarity comes a new code for you to play the game of work-life.

For most of my career, I had lived a significant amount of my waking life living with the tension of Work-life Disorder. The day I overcame obstacle #5 was like a new dawn and awakening. After years living most of my time, most days each week with the stress, suck, or saga routine. The sky cleared, and a new day was born. On this new day, I could clearly see for the first time I was spending the time in my work-life in no place I really wanted to be.

I also recognized how exhausted I had become. Something I never paid attention to before. I had lived decades playing the counting game surrounded by people with big bank accounts and swimming pools. And playing the counting game in those crowds was all about the hustle and the grind. It was expected to work several continuous weeks for six or seven days each week. And if ever a time discomfort was expressed, all I got told back was more the same. I was told to work even harder because what mattered most was making money. I am not judging that work-life priority being first because, for some, that's true. But my priority was different. And for the first time, I was able to breathe articulable confidence in what I felt inside. Remember, my whisper? *"Do you, be Dave's Disorder."* After using it to discover my Want-Day-Do and prioritizing it, I finally could see why, no matter what I did for years, I never found my ideal work-life. Instead, I was being subservient to the priorities of others. My prioritized Want-Day-Do said what mattered to me was meaning first. Meaning that is found in adventure and being authentic. Meaning to me like the unrepeatable fingerprint on my hand. I had carried the tension of Work-life Disorder for so long that I accepted it. The most freeing part for me was discovering rule # 6 and # 7 in my code. My code contained details how to play the game of work-life like no other could play. And through its authenticity, my code freed me from ever again thinking or feeling my work-life was less important than any other. But to use it, I still needed to escape, and like you, two remaining obstacles still stood in my way.

Before we go into the final act of this game, it is important to pause, regroup, and consider. You may have started your journey a few days ago. Or you may be like Nick, who spent a few months, or like Cali, who spent over a year to arrive where you are now. The length of time it has taken you to arrive at this point in the game is not significant to your ability to escape. But what you have already accomplished to arrive where you are now is. You have proven to yourself there is more you want from the time you live your waking life at work. You decided to make the uncomfortable turn away from Cerberus. You persisted through the fear, comfort, or frustration focused on keeping you contained. You fought off the madness that kept telling you it is better for you to remain more the same. You then courageously looked down a path that may have felt cold and was too dark to see. Yet, you decided to move and overcome the obstacles in your way. All while teaching yourself how to breathe, believe, and consider yourself in new ways. You then faced and moved through The Work-life Disorder. A disorder that constantly caused you to be caught in the middle between where you felt you must and wanted to be. So, before we move and face the last two obstacles in this game, I must say out loud, good job. You have chosen to move a long way for yourself and the people, places, and things you care for most. A distance that may make facing the remaining two obstacles ahead the hardest and scariest. I only say that to ensure you don't detach from the reality seen from the journeys of many before. The reality that has been more the same across many. The reality that The Work-Life Escape Room becomes harder and harder until you escape. With all that in mind.

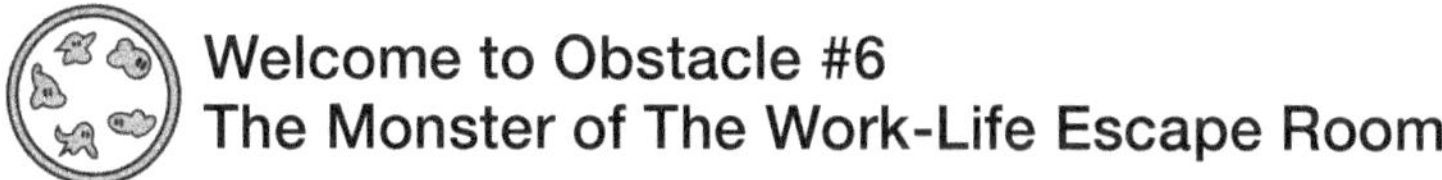

Welcome to Obstacle #6
The Monster of The Work-Life Escape Room

Before you face the monster, here are a few upfront details you must know and are explained in more detail below:

1. You cannot fight your monster. Instead, you must tame it.

2. Don't expect your monster to tell you to move past it or give you 100% permission to do so.

3. The number of people who were able to engage and interact with their monster only one time to tame it can be counted on one human hand. The reality is it may take several times, for several weeks or months. And although it has only happened in some cases so far, taming your monster in order to move past it may take a year or more.

The monster in The Work-life Escape Room is not any monster; it is one of the toughest monsters you, me, and many may ever face. This monster has beaten every type of work-life from millionaires, executives, directors, managers, and many others such as those who worked on the front lines. This monster has shown itself in many ways. And this 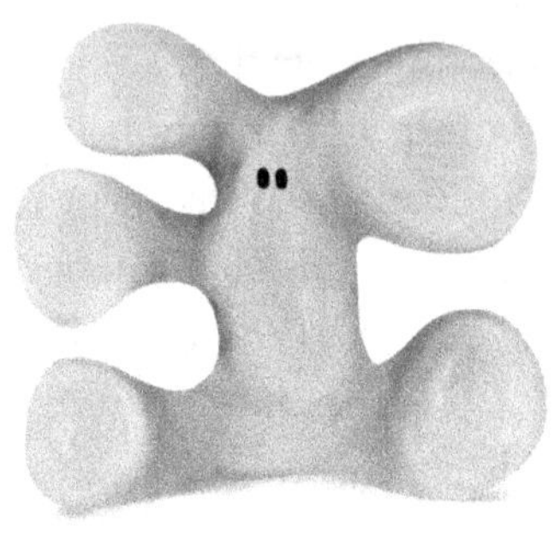 monster is responsible for convincing many to choose to stay. The problem you face is not the monsters from others in the past but the monster you face today. This monster you already know all too well. This monster is your current life. So you can't kill it and instead must discover how to tame it.

Taming the monster in The Work-life Escape Room has meant many different things to many people. For Richard, that meant facing his life and finding an agreement with it where he could move to a different country.  For Kelley, it meant having a conversation with her boss's boss to report the hidden abuses that had prevented her from spending the time in her current work-life getting what she wanted most of the time. For Valerie, that meant going back to school to get promoted. For Deon, that meant going through a divorce and moving into a completely new industry.

For the work-lives that codified the contents for this book, no two monsters were alike. However, there were common clues found across those who were able to overcome them. The first of which admittedly caught me more by surprise than many others. It was the idea that it is best to talk with your monster versus fight with it. I must admit it feels awkward for me to say such an idea caught me by surprise. But I feel compelled to share with you my experience in the slim chance you find yourself feeling like I did. I hope it helps you know, no matter what your monster is made of, if you choose, you can tame it. My monster represented years full of events and choices that were made up of hurt, guilt, despair, regret, and disappointment. And I didn't want anything more to do with it. I wanted to be done with it. I had my whisper, I had my prioritized Want-Day-Do, and I finally had the clarity to see what

I really wanted. Yet, at this stage of the game, I found myself facing the life I had made. A life I couldn't overcome in my mind. And because of that, I share with you in sincere vulnerability. During my journey to escape The Work-Life Escape Room, I danced several times and made a few significant attempts to end it all. But I, like many before, was missing an important clue. A clue that pointed to something I needed before facing the monster in the room.

Before any of us face our monster, we must distill what we want in our prioritized Want-Day-Do into "I want statements." This is because we must say what we want to see in order to see what we want to be. To help you get started, let me provide you with examples of some of mine. *"I want to express my true voice," "I want to help others find and free their true voice," "I want to help others free themselves from the tensional space that keeps them living with Work-life Disorder," "I want to lend and not borrow," and "I want to own my space and time."* This part of addressing obstacle #6 wasn't hard for many because it is mostly placing the words "I want" in front of each item of your prioritized Want-Day-Do. But "I want statements" are required. Without them you will not escape. What comes next has mostly shown to be anything but easy.

Telling the monster what you want has been viewed by many as a complex challenge. Some have reflected that having the conversations felt like fighting multiple battles simultaneously. For instance, Paul's, prioritized Want-Day-Do suggested his ideal work-life was more like a freelance type of work-life. This sharply contrasted with his job at the bank and was said to be obnoxiously inappropriate in the eyes of his partner Tim, whom he recently married, and to both his and Tim's parents. This was because what Paul said he wanted seemed foreign to what they all knew. During our conversations, Paul expressed frustration because it wasn't until facing this obstacle that he started to believe he could not escape. Paul shared this stage of the game caused him so much stress he felt he was damned if he did and damned if he didn't. Others shared that facing their monster felt like facing double standards. This was the case for Joanna, whose monster was made up of expectations from her parents, friends, and the industry she worked in for over a decade. Joanna shared how she felt she couldn't overcome how unsupported she felt by her friends, family, and colleagues, who largely made up the people, places, and things she cared for most. She shared how these important people in her life felt it was okay for others to move on to different ways of spending time at work, but how dare she feel that way. Having achieved great success over the past 12 years, she knew moving away from that direction would be seen as a mistake by the important people in her life. And there were people like Bill, whose monster he found was the guilt he placed on himself. And Leo, whose monster was in a relationship

with someone not technically considered his partner but someone very close in his life. Many have been successful taming their monsters and some like Paul, were convinced by it to stay. What about Joanna, Bill, and Leo? Joanna overcame her monster by completely disengaging and moving to a new state. Bill, similar to me, gave himself a binary ultimatum. In other words, he told himself he would move forward or be done with his life. And to his surprise, Leo found his monster was made up in his mind. The organization of his "I want statements" was welcomed and received warmly by his partner. Bill found that he thought he was always telling his partner what he wanted to do with the time in his work-life, but it was never conveyed in a way she could grab on to. The monster in the room is made up of many different things. It is up to you how you choose for it to be tamed. But however you do, you must move past it.

If you pause for a moment and look over your prioritized Want-Day-Do, aren't its contents mostly things you have always known? But over time, you have placed those wants aside just like I and many did, too. Not for just one right reason, but many. Reason after reason, rationalized and justified. This is why the door you now stand in front of seems unfathomable and what's beyond unimaginable.

Welcome to Obstacle #7 — The Final Door to Escape.

When you look at the door, you will see near the top a little sign that says, "No re-entry." And in a place you would not expect to find are words near the bottom that say, "push to open." The obstacle in your way is in the space between. For you to escape the room, you must open this door. A door that was pushed shut by those in society whose stories, standards, and stigmas dictate it is best to remain. And by the friends and family who keep it shut because they want more of the same. Indeed what stands in front of you is not an easy thing to move. But open it you must, if you wish to leave the room.

To open the final door, you must expect much more for yourself. You must expect today to be the "best day ever" most of the time, most days each week. And no longer wait for one day someday you may never live to see. To get this expectancy you must find a treat. A treat that is hidden,

but is within your reach. The treat you must find is known as pie. And if you wish to escape you must choose to eat it today and during most of the time remaining in your work-life.

If you choose to eat pie, here is what you must do:

> **Permission:** The first thing you must do is chew and swallow your permission. Permission that says you get to have all the things in your prioritized Want-Day-Do including all the things you once let hide.

> **Immersion:** Next, you must intentionally immerse yourself in this permission. You must do this so you can say and see all the things you want to be in the remaining time of your work-life.

> **Energy:** Finally, by enacting this permission and immersion, you will find the critical source of energy needed to escape and remain free from The Work-life Escape Room.

It's now time for you to make your final choice. Will you choose to eat PIE to get the energy needed to open the final door, or choose to stay and begin making your way back to Cerberus? No choice is wrong, and no choice is right. But the choice you make will determine how your time will be spent in most of your remaining work-life.

When you start eating PIE every day, you will find yourself living in a place many say is impossible. A place where the time you live your life at work brings you what you really want most of the time, most days each week. The things that authentically make you happy, inspired or fulfilled. All that remains now is for you to say you are ready.

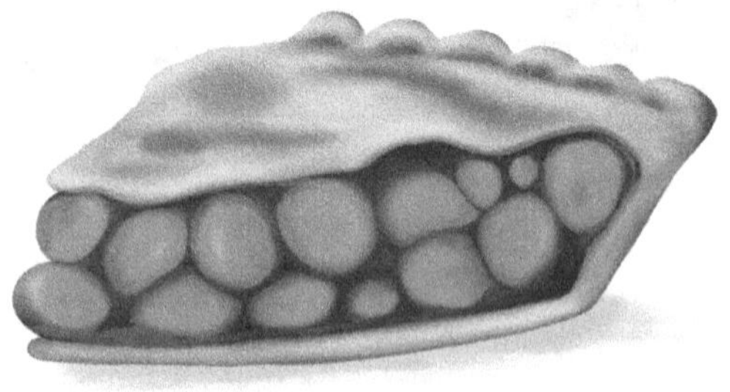

I AM READY

I AM READY TO BE ME,
I AM READY TO BE MY WHISPER,
I AM READY TO LIVE A WORK LIFE VERY FEW
CONSIDER,
SO TODAY I SAY IS THE DAY I MAKE,
THE DAY I SEE MYSELF ESCAPE,
AND WITH IT I COME TO BE,
LIVING MY LIFE AS AN IMPOSSIBILITY.

In my send-off to you, I would like to end the way I began, by asking you a question.

What do you have that no one else can or ever will?

This question is important because it exposes what is best about each of our lives. A question answered by two simple words: your fingerprint. Something with you every day symbolic of the unrepeatable person you are authentically and the impossibility you could be.

The Work-Life Escape Room was never a story to be a story; it is a reflection of what was real in life, connected. For many, their eyes were taught to look at work in a direction where seeing anything other than the stress, suck, or saga routine most of the time, most days each week, was a little ridiculous or radical. My story was similar. Much of my work-life was found subservient to manipulative puppetry used by insecurities, egos, and power-hungry people. Many of those individuals rationalized their greedy actions, while others restrained, enslaved, or beat up people, saying what they were doing was "what was best for business." Despite their actions, it was common to hear them proclaim they held real care and concern for doing what was best for others. For decades, I listened and followed everything they said to do and be. And my story didn't change until the day I broke and could no longer breathe. This leads me to give you just one more thing. Something the late Paul Harvey might subscribe as *"The rest of the story…."*

The day I saw The Work-life Escape Room, I could never unsee its obvious, oblivious reality. That day, I became embarrassed and ashamed. When I looked around, I could see my friends and colleagues had many impressive things. This was because they played the counting game to the fullest. I, on the other hand, felt deeply unhappy, uninspired, and unfulfilled. I wanted something different.

What stood in my way was not my inability, it was a choice. So, I changed my choice and decided to escape. It meant I had to find the pieces of me I had tucked away yet yearned to breathe and be most of the time, most days each week. I had to rediscover what I really wanted, get my shit together, and choose this day. A day where you are reading the book I never intended to write. Living most of my time in a day I once believed was impossible for me. So thank you. Thank you for reading my book, and for the privilege of accompanying you through this journey.

Today is also the day you have made—a day I hope you continue to choose for the rest of your work-life. A day determined by what you choose to say you want to see. And what you see, by what you dare to be.

About the Illustrator

Christina Carlson has a unique gift for visualizing the brilliance and ideas of leaders worldwide. Her experience as a facilitator and trainer, conversationalist and coach, speaker and artist allows her to bring the vision and innovation of leaders to the rest of the world. The opportunity to illustrate and design this book has been a privilege and a journey she will never forget. You can connect with her at https://whatsupunstuck.com.

About the Author

My belief is as humans, we are more the same than different, uniquely unrepeatable, better together, and our best comes from when we enact love, care, and concern for one another. My passion is focused on the performance of human potential at work. My priority is to help cure Work-life Disorder. My commitment is in service to all these things as I serve as a Lecturer at Boston University and while being in Senior Executive Roles.

Appendix

Choice #1—The Choice to Stay or Move

Choosing to move is first a choice to turn away from Cerberus. This is not an easy thing to do. In fact, in reflection of myself and hundreds before you, this choice is one of the hardest in the room. But remember:

Rule #3   Where you look is where you can choose to move and go.

So if more than a good enough work-life is what you want, choosing to turn is the choice you must make.

To help you do this, here is the summary of steps that have helped many of us before:

1. Go to a mirror in your house or find one you can hold in your hand.

2. Now, look at yourself and think about what you want most from the time in your waking life.

As you may soon recognize, there is a good chance you will find yourself, like many of us before, unable to say or see yourself having what you really want most of the time. Things you hold authentically true deep inside that find you happy, inspired, or fulfilled. The good news is at this stage of the game, all you need to do is turn, and you can do this without being able to see or say any of this. Remember...

Rule #4   If you don't write it down and say it out loud, whatever it is will never come true.

3. Use the adjacent page to write down or say to yourself "The time of my life is worth more to me than what I am spending it on in my current work-life."

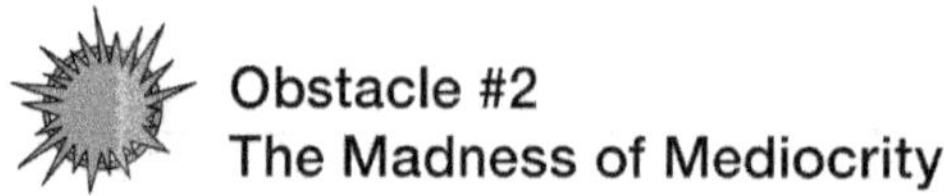 **Obstacle #2**
The Madness of Mediocrity

Finding your whisper and other things you will need to find to escape The Work-Life Escape Room will require you look for and find clues.

Finding clues to help you find your whisper starts by:

1. Think about a time in your life you can say with no hesitation you were happy, inspired or fulfilled.

2. Now, think a little deeper about that time. What about that time was authentic to what you really want deep inside?

3. Now, think about a time when you were just being you? No, not the made-up you that you have played as much of your work-life, the real you.

4. Finally, think about what it meant to be the real you. During that time didn't you feel free and alive? Living in a time of your life that felt light, fun, and effortless.

Use the adjacent page to journal your thoughts.

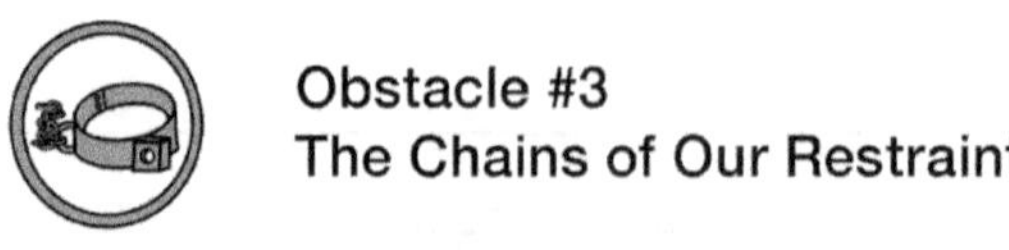

**Obstacle #3
The Chains of Our Restraint**

Here are the steps to unlock the lock:

1. Believe in your whisper, the one you may feel is true inside, knowing you will most likely be unable to see how it can be a lived reality for you most of the time.

2. Make a bet on that belief.

3. Commit to your bet on that belief even though you cannot see how getting it is possible.

Use the adjacent page to journal your thoughts.

If you do these three things, the lock will open.

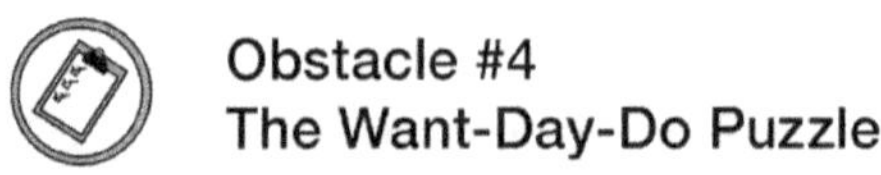

Steps to use the Jar of Work-Life Struggle:

1. Imagine a jar or, as do as some have before, go and get some type of physical jar.

2. Then, write out any and all work-life struggles on anything that can capture your writing and be put in the jar. It has been common to see people use paper, sticky pads, and napkins.

Use the text box to capture your list, if needed.

To complete the Want-Day-Do puzzle, use the adjacent blank space and complete the following:

1. Write everything you want from your ideal work-life. As you do, please remember:

Rule #4   If you don't write it down and say it out loud, whatever it is will never become in your lived reality.

2. Now, in the space below, describe what your ideal day would look like. And yes, this includes the time before and after any "official" time you spent at work.

3. Finally, on the designated worksheet made available in the book or on a new piece of paper, space on a tablet, or other writing surface, describe what you want to do at work and the way you want to do it.

With this complete, let's now address any limitations you have placed in your solution for the Want-Day-Do puzzle.

1. Review your list and highlight anything that is less than "What would you do if nothing was impossible?"

2. Review your list and think about anything you didn't put on it because you couldn't see how to get it. If you discover anything, write it in!

3. For each item in your list, add two additional descriptors to each:

   a) What does each item mean to you? A way this has been productively accomplished was to describe how each item would be explained to someone else.

   b) What does each item look like in any given day you would say exist in your ideal work-life?

Use the adjacent page to journal your thoughts.

Obstacle #5
The Priority of Our Priorities Puzzle

1. In the space below, write out predictability, money, and meaning. And do so in a way that will allow you to either place tally numbers below each word or write out the items you are accounting for each type.

2. Now, associate each item in your Want-Day-Do with one or
   more categories listed in the Priority of our Priorities puzzle.

Remember...

Rule #1 & #2   No choice is right or wrong, and fairness is not
                     real. It is either authentic to you, or it is not.

3. Now, complete a weighting exercise based on the number of
   times you associated items from your Want-Day-Do to each of
   the Priorities of our Priorities categories.

For example, my weighted grouping found 33 items from my
Want-Day-Do placed in the meaning priority. I had another 11
items placed in the money priority. And finally, I had three items
placed in the predictability priority. In my example, my work-life
priorities meant I mostly needed to find meaning in the time I
spent at work, followed by money, and the lowest of my priorities
was predictability. Some have been the same, and others are
different.

The point is not what combination you hold. The point is to get
your shit together so you can finish getting the code to unlock
your ideal work-life. One where most of the time you live your life
at work brings you what you really want.

Obstacle #6
The Monster of The Work-Life Escape Room

Before you face the monster, here are a few upfront details you must know:

You cannot fight your monster. Instead, you must tame it.

Don't expect your monster to tell you to move past it or give you 100% permission to do so.

The number of people who were able to engage and interact with their monster only one time to tame it can be counted on one human hand. The reality is it may take several times for several weeks or months, and while it has only occurred in some cases, it may even take a year or more.

1. You must distill what you want in your prioritized Want-Day-Do into "I want statements."

> To help you get started, let me provide you with examples of some of mine:
> "I want to express my true voice,"
> "I want to help others find and free their true voice,"
> "I want to help others free themselves from the tensional space that keeps them living with Work-life Disorder,"
> "I want to lend and not borrow," and
> "I want to own my space and time."

The monster in the room is made up of many different things. It is up to you how you choose for it to be tamed. But however you do, you must move past it.

Obstacle #7
The Final Door to Escape.

When you look at the door, you will see near the top a little sign that says, "No re-entry." And in a place you would not expect to find are words near the bottom that say, "push to open." The obstacle in your way is in the space between. For you to escape, you must open this door.

To open the final door, you must expect much more for yourself. You must expect today to be the "best day ever" most of the time, most days each week. And no longer wait for one day someday you may never live to see.

To get this expectancy you must find a treat. A treat that is hidden, but is within your reach. The treat you must find is known as pie. And if you wish to escape you must choose to eat it today and during most of the time remaining in your work-life.

If you choose to eat pie, here is what you must do:

1. **Permission:** The first thing you must do is chew and swallow your permission. Permission that says you get to have all the things in your prioritized Want-Day-Do including all the things you once let hide.

2. **Immersion:** Next, you must intentionally immerse yourself in this permission. You must do this so you can say and see all the things you want to be in the remaining time of your work-life.

3. **Energy:** Finally, by enacting this permission and immersion, you will find the critical source of energy needed to escape and remain free from The Work-life Escape Room.

Use the adjacent page to journal your thoughts.

What would you do if nothing was impossible?